2025 K-CONSUMER TREND INSIGHTS

KB193072

First published in the Republic of Korea in October, 2024 by Miraebook Publishing Co.

Inquiries should be addressed to
Miraebook Publishing Co.
5th Fl., Miraeui-chang Bldg., 62-1 Jandari-ro, Mapo-ku, Seoul
Tel : 82-2-325-7556 / email : ask@miraebook.co.kr

www.miraebook.co.kr
blog.naver.com/miraebookjoa
Instagram.com/miraebook
Facebook.com/miraebook

ISBN 978 89 5989 725 4 13320

2025
K-CONSUMER
TREND
INSIGHTS

Rando Kim · Miyoung Jeon · Jihye Choi · Jung Yoon Kwon ·
Dahye Han · Hyewon Lee · June Young Lee · Hyang Eun Lee · Yelin Chu ·
Dahyen Jeon · Naeun Kim · YouHyun Alex Suh · Proofread by Michel Lamblin

미래의창

SNAKE SENSE

An era that demands a keen sense as sharp as a snake's. What will you preserve, and what will you change?

Will you keep it, or will you change it?

There are two ways to navigate the world: preserve or change. Japan tends to preserve, when necessary, fulfilling its traditional responsibilities. It's common for a son who once held an executive position in a major company to quit and return home to run his family's small countryside restaurant after his father passes away. Perhaps that's why in Japan, it's not unusual to find family businesses that have been around for 100 or 200 years, or artisans who have dedicated their lives to a single craft.

In contrast, South Korea is poised for change. What might a small-town restaurant owner say if someone suggested that their son take over the business? Perhaps something along the lines of: "Are you serious? My son is an executive at a huge conglomerate! I worked all my life at this restaurant to ensure my children wouldn't have to."

So, which is better, preserving or changing? Both have their merits, though it's more accurate to say each has its pros and cons rather than claiming one is superior. In the analog era, the answer is "preserve"; in the digital era, it's "change."

By the late 1980s, Japan led the world. The Empire State Building in Manhattan, a symbol of the United States, was under Japanese ownership. The secret to Japan's success was its unmatched manufacturing industry, passed down through generations of skilled craftsmen. These artisans excelled in precision, outdoing others in cutting, shaping, and assembling countless parts. Proverbs like "He that hunts two hares catches neither한 우물을 파라" and "A rolling stone gathers no moss" reflect the value of preserving in an analog-driven economy.

But in the digital age, things have shifted. The last 30 years, marked by the rise of the internet, smartphones, platforms, and AI, have brought relentless technological change. Competitiveness now lies in those who adapt best. Japan, with its deep-rooted traditions, is slower to change. They still use faxes and stamps. There are even stories of someone emailing to confirm if a fax was received, or of inventing a "stamp robot" instead of eliminating the need for stamps. What was once a strength in the analog economy now holds them back in the digital age.

Meanwhile, South Korea has embraced change. With the slogan, "We were late to industrialization, but let's lead in the information age," the country pursued digitalization and readily shifted to new business models. As a result, the gap between Korea and Japan has narrowed, and by some measures, Korea has even pulled ahead. In 2024, Korea's gross national income per capita will be $36,194, surpassing Japan by $401. Household net assets will also exceed Japan's by $3,500, at $186,100.

Culturally, the same pattern holds. In the 1990s, Japanese pop music was dominant, with many secretly listening to rock group X-Japan despite their being banned in Korea. Now, K-pop stars like Blackpink and BTS have overtaken J-pop. How? While Japan, with its strong domestic market, continues to focus on preserving its CD-based industry, Korean musicians went global, leveraging platforms like YouTube.

National power has various aspects, and there are several indicators in both the economy and culture, so there is no need for us to make a fuss about being better off than Japan. The shift we're seeing is, in part, due to the difference between preservation and change. As markets shift from physical CDs to digital platforms like YouTube, from CRT TVs to OLEDs, from internal combustion engines to EVs, and from comic books to webtoons, companies that embrace continuous innovation have risen to world-class status. They've done so by not hesitating to change.

This is not just a challenge for nations or companies, but for individuals as well. Since COVID-19, our environment has been changing even faster. How we respond to these shifts will determine whether we sink slowly or leap forward. There are many valuable things we must protect, but if forced to choose, we are living in an era where change takes precedence.

Consumer Trends in a Time of Uncertainty

"Is it just me who's struggling?"

This is a common question these days. While the national economy may not look bad on paper, business is slow, and life feels tough. Exports are propping up economic indicators thanks to a strong exchange rate, but the domestic economy is sluggish. Rising costs are mainly to blame. Labor costs are up, interest rates are high, and import prices are steep due to the high exchange rate. Rent remains inflated from the post-COVID real estate boom. As consumer spending tightens, small business owners are hit hard. In 2023, the National Tax Service reported 1 million business closures, the largest number since records began in 2006. Declining sales, driven by weak consumer sentiment, are the main cause.

So, what's the economic outlook for the second half of 2024 and for 2025? Will things improve? Unfortunately, no major rebound is expected. 2025 is projected to be a flat year with no substantial growth or decline. In the U.S. – the driver of the global economy – growth rates, unemployment, retail sales, and industrial output are all stable, but show little promise of a major upswing. Thankfully, the risk of an unexpected crisis also seems low. Korea's economy is likely to follow suit – stable, but with little growth momentum. While some export sectors remain strong, the domestic economy will continue to struggle with sluggish consumption.

What are the trends during this stagnation? In such times, the focus shifts to small movements in the present. However, trends don't stop altogether; technological advances and shifts in population continue to drive significant changes. When analyzing consumption trends during this stagnation, it's essential to keep both these perspectives in mind.

I would like to summarize the top 10 keywords for 2025 in three categories: (1) central trends, (2) micro trends born from economic stagnation, and (3) macro trends driven by changes in population, technology, and the environment.

This year's central keyword is "omnivore." Today's consumers no longer follow traditional group norms based on age, gender, income, or region. Instead, they base their consumption on personal lifestyles, tastes, and identities. The gap in consumption behavior between groups is narrowing, while the gap between individuals is widening. This omnivore trend may seem straightforward, but it challenges our assumptions about consumers and markets, making it a critical shift.

Small shifts in consumer behavior, amplified in a stagnant economy, are called "micro trends." In 2025, we expect these to be particularly prominent. Rather than pursuing grand ambitions, people will find satisfaction in a problem-free day (#VeryOrdinaryDay). This will lead to preferences for small, harmless things (harmlessness) and an approach to self-improvement focused on incremental gains (one-point-up). To cater to these subtle shifts, businesses must offer a series of small, personalized improvements – like adding toppings to a pizza – rather than aiming for big, sweeping changes (toppings economy).

Even in a sluggish economy, structural shifts driven by technology, climate, population, and market dynamics continue, and in fact, they are accelerating. These are what we call "macro trends." New macro trends include the evolving concept of "K-culture" as global mobility increases (Gradation K), the growing "climate sensitivity" due to climate change, the "appeal of materiality" as a reaction against virtual technologies, "face tech" that humanizes technology, and "coevolution strategies," which highlight the interconnectedness of market ecosystems.

The Unique Adaptability of Snakes

2025 is the year of the Blue Snake. Traditionally, snakes evoke fear due to their slithering form and venomous fangs. They also carry associations with evil, as in the story of Adam and Eve. However, snakes are also revered for their symbolism of abundance, fertility, and wisdom. In Korean culture, snakes are believed to protect wealth, and they frequently appear in symbols of healing and medicine.

Snakes are incredibly adaptable creatures. They shed their skin to grow and hibernate to survive the cold. This adaptability has profound meaning for us in an era of constant environmental change. To thrive, we too must adapt and innovate, growing through the painful process of shedding old ways and responding to the shifting world around us.

Snakes excel at detecting subtle changes in their environment. They use their highly developed senses to survive – smelling through their tongues, sensing heat, detecting ground vibrations, and seeing in the dark. This acute awareness allows them to respond quickly and effectively to threats and opportunities.

We can learn from this. In times of upheaval, we must tap into all our senses and instincts to detect changes and seize new opportunities. For 2025, this acute, snake-like awareness is crucial, which is why the English keyword title for the year is "Snake Sense." Let's face the challenges of the year with the keen perception of a snake.

While this may be taken anecdotally, I have observed that many individuals around me are grappling with feelings of depression these days. Age seems irrelevant, affecting both the young and middle-aged alike. Their distress is not necessarily attributable to the challenges of securing employment or the difficulties of running a business; rather, it appears to stem from a discord between heightened expectations and the harshness of reality. Our daily encounters with smartphones, laden with images of a seemingly perfect life, can exacerbate our own feelings of inadequacy. Although the standard of living has improved compared to the past, our emotional well-being has become increasingly fragile as a result. We find ourselves ensnared in a relentless cycle of comparison.

For those who resonate with the sentiments expressed in the preceding paragraph, I wish to illuminate the underlying meanings of "#VeryOrdinaryDay" and "one-point-up" within this book. The lives showcased on social media are often significantly embellished, creating an illusion that can lead to envy. Ironically, the very individuals we admire may also experience feelings of inferiority when they encounter our posts. We live in an era characterized by a peculiar paradox: individuals cultivate envy towards one another, thereby fostering a pervasive sense of defeatism in an all vs. all world. This phenomenon persists even for those who do not engage heavily with social media, as we perpetually measure ourselves against others, compelled by no one but ourselves, and consequently suffer from the burden of unmet expectations.

It is imperative that we cease this cycle of comparison and redirect our focus toward our own small daily lives. If we manage to navigate a day without significant difficulties in this tumultuous world, that alone signifies our success: we have lived a #VeryOrdinaryDay. The significance of small daily moments cannot be overstated; they are not only invaluable but also immensely empowering. "True nobility is not found in surpassing others, but in surpassing oneself from the past." There is no need for grandiosity. If you discover a modest "one point" that represents an improvement over yesterday, that holds intrinsic value. It is never too late; you are not lagging behind. If you aspire to move a mountain, begin by carrying small stones.

September 2024,

Rando Kim

(lead author)

SNAKE SENSE

CONTENTS

Savoring a Bit of Everything:
Omnivores

An omnivore is traditionally defined as an organism that eats both plants and animals, but it also has a broader meaning: "having diverse interests." In sociology, the concept refers to a person with a wide range of cultural tastes, unconfined by any specific culture. We would like to expand this further, referring to consumers who create their own consumption styles and defy stereotypes as "omnivores." Modern omnivores don't follow the characteristics of groups classified by traditional demographic criteria but instead display unique consumption patterns shaped by their individuality and interests.

The rise of omnivores is closely tied to increased life expectancy. With longer lives, people feel a greater need to build new "life portfolios." We now see more generations coexisting than ever before, with social media facilitating intergenerational exchanges.

As a result, the marketing concept of segments based on demographic criteria is being fundamentally challenged. The omnivore trend calls for individual approaches that consider new variables like values, tastes, moods, and situations. Markets and organizations are no longer "typical." It's time to discard old stereotypes and rethink conventional wisdom. Start fresh and reconsider all assumptions!

옴니보어

"Oh, I was going to watch the original broadcast, but the baby woke up ⟨sad face emoji⟩. I'll have to watch it later when it's uploaded."

"Tomorrow is a day off, so I'm going to 'run' all night!"

"I'm using my vacation days to binge watch, haha"

In the open chatroom for the webtoon-based drama *Lovely Runner*선재업고뛰어, which is set primarily in a high school, hundreds of fans of the drama's protagonist, Sun-jae, gather to chat. While they discuss the drama without knowing each other's faces or names, glimpses of their daily lives emerge. A mother raising a young child, a college student juggling schoolwork, an office worker who enjoys binge-watching… Despite differences in age, profession, and location, fans of all generations seamlessly connect through their shared love for the drama. This reflects modern life, where personal interests transcend traditional group labels like "thirty-something," "woman," or "office worker."

But this is only part of the picture. Many live lives that defy the stereotypes associated with their social groups: a 50-year-old manager on parental leave, a high school student earning pocket money through a smart store, a 30-year-old woman who lives for weekend futsal games, or a wealthy individual shopping at Daiso for YouTube-recommended items. The stereotypes we associate with age, gender, and profession are fading. Notions like "acting your age" or "being masculine/feminine" are becoming outdated. The sight of people of all ages gathering in hobby-based clubs and politely addressing one another by their first names (rather than by last names or hierarchical forms of addressing common in Korean social situations) highlights that we now live in a time when shared interests matter more than demographic traits.

When analyzing the market, narrowing down the target consumer group based on demographic characteristics such as age, gender, occupation, residential area, education level, and income, is known as "market segmentation." Each group identified through this process is called a "segment." For instance, generational categories like "X," "Millennial," "Z," and "Alpha" are commonly used segments in consumer classification. Segmentation has been a foundational concept in marketing because it assumes that consumers within a segment share similar lifestyles, values, and tastes. However, as individual preferences become increasingly diverse, the differences between groups are shrinking, while the differences between individuals are growing. Even within the same Millennial generation, people display completely different tastes and consumption behaviors.

The term "omnivore" carries a derivative meaning of "having a broad range of interests." In sociology, an omnivore is someone with diverse cultural tastes, not bound by any single culture. We would like to take this further by describing consumers who defy stereotypes and create their own consumption styles as "omnivores." Modern omnivores don't adhere to the traits of groups defined by traditional demographic criteria; instead, they exhibit distinct consumption patterns shaped by their individuality and interests.

Omnivores are not rare or unusual. They represent a growing trend observed in everyday life. Let's explore how conventional stereotypes related to life stages, age, generation, and gender are being disrupted.

An Omnivore's World

The "right time" fallacy: Mixed life cycles

Postnatal care centers, daycare centers, kids' cafes, and elementary school entrance ceremonies are places where parents with young children are met with a surprising trend: the ages of parents with children of the same age now range widely, from parents in their twenties to those in their fifties. With more people delaying childbirth, reactions like "I thought I'd be the oldest, but I was surprised I wasn't" or "I was shocked to be the youngest" have become increasingly common. According to data from Shinhan Card's Big Data Research Institute, the age distribution of those visiting kids' cafes has shifted. Over the two years up to the first half of 2024, visits by patrons in their 40s and 50s-to-60s rose by 1.7% and 6.7%, while visits by people in their 20s and 30s dropped by 6.9% and 1.5%, respectively. Among the 50s-to-60s segment were not only parents who had children later in life but also grandparents who became caregivers early. This mix of ages in the childcare space reflects the reality of today's diverse family structures. It's no longer possible to predict a parent's age based solely on the age of their child.

The shifting life cycle is also evident in the workplace. Childcare leave, once primarily taken by associates and managers, is now being used by deputy managers and even higher-ranking employees. Additionally, it's becoming harder to predict the age of new hires. A survey of 897 people by the job site Incruit found that the average age of new employees is now 29.4 for men and 27.6 for women. With extended periods of education and job preparation, and the rise of "second-hand new employees" with experience from multiple jobs, people are entering the workforce closer to age 30. Reflecting this shift, seven out of ten respondents in a previous survey said that upper age limits for new hires are unnecessary, and many companies are already removing age restrictions during recruitment. Both employees and companies now recognize that there is no established "right time" to begin a career.

The idea that "there's a time for studying" is also losing relevance. It's no longer unusual to see people in their thirties enrolling in undergraduate programs to switch careers, or others

pursuing graduate studies while working or even after retirement. Universities are adapting to these demographic changes.
Yeongsan University in Busan, where 22.6% of the population
was over 65 as of 2023, has launched a senior modeling department aimed at the older generation. This is the first full four-year
undergraduate program of its kind, offering not only practical
training but also liberal arts courses in the humanities.

The overlapping of life cycles is also straining household
finances. In the past, old age was seen as a time when children
would support their parents, but now many seniors find themselves financially supporting both their children and parents,
even after reaching 65, the socially recognized "elderly age."
According to Statistics Korea's *Survey on the Status of the Elderly,* only 0.9% of people aged 65 and older reported regularly
providing financial support to their children in 2011. By 2020,
this number soared to 12.5%. Moreover, the 2020 Social Survey
found that 60.3% of respondents aged 65-69 said their children
were helping with their parents' living expenses.

Why you shouldn't ignore them just because they're young: Age reversal

A song called the *"Maratanghulu* Challenge" topped TikTok
Music and became the #1 most popular song on Instagram Reels
within a month of its video being posted on April 17, 2024. The
challenge quickly went viral, with participation from famous
creators and celebrities alike. The song's addictive lyrics and

melody became so catchy that it was dubbed the "new earworm song banned for the college entrance exam," owing to its extreme catchiness and potential to disrupt students' studying and test-taking. Curiosity grew around the creator behind this wildly popular challenge, and when people found out who it was, they were shocked: the creator, Suh Eve, was born in 2012 – a 12-year-old elementary school student. Her taller-than-average height, talent at dancing, and high-quality video production made it hard to believe she was so young, surprising many who had assumed otherwise.

Another example of this age reversal is the account "The Sound of Peeling a Tangerine귤 까먹는 소리" (@cook_gyuri10), which amassed 152,000 followers in just a year with videos solely focused on cooking. The main character expertly prepares dishes like radish and soybean paste stew, *oyakodon*, and soufflé pancakes with the finesse of a seasoned chef. Anyone watching would assume the creator is an experienced office worker living alone. However, confusion sets in when the videos reveal a young voice worrying about school performance evaluations or looking forward to the lunch menu, even though her face remains hidden. In reality, the account is run by Kim Gyu-ri, a second-year middle school student. Creators like these, who showcase talents far beyond their years, are often called "god-babies," with many viewers humorously reflecting on their own abilities – or lack thereof – in comparison.

The assumption that young people neglect preparing for their future is a common misconception. While foods like *malatang* and *tanghulu* might come to mind when thinking of the eating habits of teens and twenty-somethings, their eating habits are actually more considered and healthier than might be expected. With the rise of the "slow aging" trend, which focuses on life-style habits that delay aging, there's been a growing awareness of issues like "blood sugar spikes," typically a concern for diabetics. Sleep optimization and nutritional supplements have also become essential areas of interest. According to a survey by the newsletter *Uppity*어피티, which polled 798 subscribers, 78.3% of respondents said they started taking nutritional supplements before turning 30, and 11% said they began before age 20. This active approach to health management is reflected in spending patterns. Data from the Shinhan Card Big Data Research Insti-tute shows that in 2023, the largest share of consumers visiting salad specialty stores and gyms were teenagers (32.5%) and twen-ty-somethings (26.9%).

In the beauty industry, slow aging has emerged as the next big trend following "anti-aging." While anti-aging focuses on preventing aging once wrinkles begin to appear, slow aging is about delaying the signs of aging as much as possible from a young age. This shift has also changed the customer base for many brands. Sulwhasoo, traditionally seen as an anti-aging brand favored by middle-aged consumers, recently joined the CJ Olive Young online mall, popular with consumers in their twenties and thirties. During a live broadcast to commemorate the launch, Sulwhasoo's signature product, "Yunjo Essence," generated sales of 700 million won in just 140 minutes. Notably, six out of ten customers who purchased the product were under thirty.

Adults who are immature: The narrowing concept of generations

When you hear the words "job experience," which generation comes to mind? You might picture young children exploring their future aspirations and aptitudes. However, in the omnivore era, that view is a stereotype. In December 2023, KidZania, a popular job experience theme park for children, hosted an adults-only event in Korea called "Kids Aniya" (meaning "I'm not a kid"), which garnered an overwhelming response from adults. With tickets available for 400 people in the afternoon to accommodate post-work schedules, they sold out quickly. Many parents even requested that the event be held in the morning after dropping their kids off at school. Due to its popularity, KidZania organized Seasons 2 and 3 of Kids Aniya in April and June 2024. Visitors left enthusiastic reviews, expressing their intent to return and experience activities they missed.

Many adults also hold onto childhood possessions long after growing up. Recently, it has become trendy for graduating high school students in the United States to carry backpacks adorned with characters from Disney and Marvel. They showcase these bags on social media, often posting photos that compare their current selves to their childhood images. Companies are capitalizing on this nostalgia by marketing products featuring beloved childhood cartoons. For instance, Lotte World hosted an event called "Detective Conan: MAGIC CITY" to coincide with the animated film's theatrical release. The event featured photo zones decorated with cartoon characters and an interactive experience space that recreated crime scenes, allowing visitors to solve mysteries around the theme park, true to the spirit of the original work. Celebrating its 30th anniversary, the original cartoon saw related merchandise sell out within just two weeks, thanks to the enthusiastic response from consumers in their twenties and thirties who are steeped in childhood nostalgia.

Additionally, Hotel Matiè Osiria in Gijang County, Busan, has introduced rooms decorated with the character Zanmang Loopy잔망루피, the famous Pororo character that has been spun-off and become a meme for mostly thirty-somethings. Since opening, the hotel has maintained an occupancy rate of over 85%, showcasing the character's strong appeal.

It is not just the youth who are bridging the generation gap. The stereotype that those aged between sixty and seventy have absolutely nothing to do with online gaming is being challenged. The e-sports team "Matagi Snipers," which has gained significant attention in Japan, boasts an average age of 67 among its players. With an official membership requirement of 65 years or older, players aged 60-64 are classified as "juniors." However, the team is not only notable for its members' ages; its slogan,

"Respected by grandchildren," reflects its competitive skill level, which rivals that of teens and twenty-somethings, the core age group for e-sports. Their main game, "Valorant," is a first-person shooter that demands quick reflexes, yet the players have demonstrated that age is no barrier with their impressive and accurate shooting.

Generational boundaries are also blurring in everyday smartphone usage. Analysis by market research service Wise-App·Retail·Goods reveals that the age gap in time spent using the YouTube app has significantly decreased over the past four years. In 2020, the group that spent the most time on YouTube – those under 20 – averaged 2,546 minutes per month, while the group that spent the least – those in their 40s – averaged just 1,067 minutes, resulting in a 2.4-fold difference. By the first half of 2024, this difference narrowed to approximately 1.7-fold, as YouTube usage increased across all age groups. Notably, the usage time among those in their 40s rose at a greater rate, further closing the gap. Mobile shopping among those aged 50 and older is also on the rise. In the first half of 2024, the number of consumers aged 50 and above using the Coupang app increased nearly threefold compared to 2019, making this age group the second largest segment of all Coupang app users, following those in their 40s.

There is no gender: A world where boundaries disappear

It is common to assume that most sports enthusiasts are men, but anyone visiting a baseball stadium these days will notice a significant change. According to the Korea Baseball Organization (KBO), 54.4% of professional baseball ticket buyers in the first half of 2024 were women, marking a 3.7 percentage point increase from the previous year. Beyond baseball, a survey by the Korea Professional Sports Association of fans in the four major sports – soccer, baseball, volleyball, and basketball – revealed a similar trend, with women comprising a growing share of the audience.

In fact, passionate female fans are increasingly knowledgeable about their teams, often knowing the players inside and out and even wearing their uniforms. The statistics reflect this enthusiasm: 63.8% of professional baseball fans, 78.4% of men's professional basketball fans, and 70.3% of women's professional volleyball fans fall into this category. Moreover, many of these women actively participate in sports themselves; the number of female amateur soccer players registered with the Korea Football Association rose by 20%, from 3,190 at the end of 2019 to 3,855 as of April 2024.

The boundaries between sports are also fading. An analysis by Hanwha General Insurance and VAIVcompany바이브컴퍼니 revealed that mentions of traditionally female-dominated activities, such as ballet and yoga, have decreased, while interest in sports that both men and women engage in, such as climbing and CrossFit, as well as high-intensity and muscle-strengthening exercises like step mill and interval training, have increased. With more women seeking to build muscle mass, the gender gap in protein-related food consumption is also narrowing. An analysis by convenience store CU showed that, in the first half of 2024, sales of protein-related products increased by 33.7% among male customers year-on-year, while female sales skyrocketed by 97.6%, indicating a significant shift.

Fashion has traditionally been a field where gender distinctions are easily identified visually. However, paradoxically, it is now at the forefront of gender integration. The rise of gender fluid or genderless fashion in recent years has seen male celebrities making headlines by embracing accessories like skirts, floral patterns, and clutch bags, typically associated with women's fashion.

Recently, the popularity of the blokecore style among women has further reinforced this genderfluid trend. "Blokecore" – a fusion of British slang for an average man, and "normcore," referring to an ordinary style – features sports uniform-inspired looks, with men wearing soccer jerseys as everyday attire. This shift has also made it more acceptable for men to wear leggings while exercising. For example, Xexymix, originally a yoga attire brand, expanded its product line to include men's wear in 2020, and by the fourth quarter of 2023, sales in this segment surged by 69% compared to the previous year.

- Omnivorous consumption that breaks
  all boundaries is on the rise.
- Let go of stereotypes!
- Go back to the basics!

#마라탕후루 #서이브
#12년생 #챌린지함께해요

출처: 이브리데이

Fashion brands are adapting to these changes by erasing gender boundaries. The brand Dunst has eliminated distinctions such as "men's jackets" and "women's shirts," opting instead to categorize items just by size (XS, S, M, L, XL). This approach allows women seeking an oversized fit to choose large sizes and men desiring a slimmer fit to select small or medium sizes, rendering gender distinctions irrelevant.

Retail spaces are also evolving. Nike Korea opened its first gender fluid store in Hongdae in 2022, setting a precedent for inclusivity. In December 2023, Lotte Department Store launched an integrated fashion hall devoid of gender distinctions in its World Mall and main branch in Busan. Similarly, Hyundai Department Store restructured its fashion division into teams focused on trends, classiness, youth, and active lifestyles, rather than adhering to traditional men's and women's categories. This shift underscores the growing importance of classifying fashion by personal taste rather than gender.

The differences in eating habits between men and women are becoming less pronounced. Traditionally, people have associated a preference for desserts and coffee with women, while men are often thought of as favoring alcohol. However, it's now common to see men seeking out trendy cafes, enjoying desserts with male friends, and even taking up baking as a hobby.

Recent changes in alcohol consumption patterns further illustrate this shift. According to an analysis of drinking behaviors from 2012 to 2021 by the Korea Disease Control and Prevention

Agency, the monthly drinking rate (representing the percentage of individuals who consumed alcohol at least once a month among those who had drunk in the past year) decreased from 85.8% to 82.2% for men, while it rose from 60.9% to 63.5% for women. Notably, the gap between men and women narrowed significantly among those in their 20s and 30s. For individuals in their 20s, the gender gap in monthly drinking rates shrank from 16.3% to 7.4%, and for those in their 30s, it decreased from 11.6% to 8.2%, bringing both figures into single digits.

A similar trend has emerged in Japan. The Hakuhodo Institute of Life and Living identified the increasing similarity in eating habits between genders as the "genderless food" phenomenon. Over a 20-year survey period, the gap in alcohol consumption between men and women also narrowed in Japan. Interestingly, the percentage of female respondents who reported enjoying cooking decreased from 46.1% in 2002 to 35.4% in 2022, while the percentage for male respondents remained steady at 27%, further closing the gap.

Given the rise of single-person households and the increasing economic participation of women in Korea, it is reasonable to assume that the "genderless food" phenomenon will continue to evolve in a similar manner.

Background of Omnivores

Why do modern individuals often consume in ways that diverge from the typical characteristics associated with their demographic groups? Several changes are driving this shift.

Firstly, increased longevity plays a significant role. As human lifespans extend, the traditional frameworks for understanding an individual's life are evolving. Professor Mauro F. Guillén, a future strategy expert and sociologist at the Wharton School, argues that the "sequential model of life," which posits that specific life tasks and lifestyles are appropriate for different life stages, is becoming outdated. Historically, society has accepted a four-stage life model: childhood characterized by play and learning, young adulthood marked by hard work, middle age focused on family support, and retirement in old age. However, with improved health and longevity, the concept of old age has expanded significantly. According to data from the World Health Organization in 2019, the healthy life expectancy in South Korea is 73.1 years. This shift makes the term "retirement" seem increasingly awkward when referring to individuals who are just 65.

In addition to the delayed life clock, the social environment has transformed. Life choices, such as education, employment, marriage, and childbirth, are increasingly seen as personal decisions rather than societal expectations, fostering an atmosphere that embraces diverse lifestyles. Moreover, rapid technological advancements make it challenging to navigate life relying solely on knowledge acquired during early years. As a result, the distinction between the learning phase and the working phase is blurry. An omnivore lifestyle, which allows individuals to start businesses in their teens while continuing their education into middle age, is becoming a natural necessity in today's world.

The increasing longevity of humans has significant implications. As we enter an era with the largest number of generations coexisting in human history, intergenerational interactions have become more prevalent. A recent micro-trend in the travel industry, known as "skip-gen travel," exemplifies this shift. Instead of busy working parents, it is often the grandparents who take their teenage grandchildren on trips. Today's grandparents, primarily baby boomers, possess the physical stamina, resources, and time to travel actively after retirement, facilitating meaningful interactions with their grandchildren.

This phenomenon is not confined to international travel; it can also be observed in Korea, where grandparents frequently engage in outings with their grandchildren or live in proximity to provide childcare support. Such intergenerational interactions contribute to the ongoing popularity of trends like "newtro," including the "granny chic" movement, where Gen Z embraces the styles of their grandmothers.

In organizational settings, generational influence is not merely top-down. Startups often showcase collaborations between CEOs in their twenties and interns in their fifties. In these environments, the young CEOs contribute innovative ideas and technical skills, while the older interns offer valuable practical experience, creating synergy within the team.

Reverse mentoring is also gaining traction in large corporations and public institutions. As the generational gap has become a significant concern in the workplace, executives and senior employees are increasingly seeking opportunities to hear insights from newer and younger team members about contemporary cultural shifts and changes in organizational dynamics. This approach is part of a broader effort to cultivate a flexible organizational culture that remains attuned to external market changes.

With the widespread use of social media, access to the diverse lifestyles of various groups has significantly increased. In the past, our understanding of others' daily lives was superficial, but now we can observe them in detail online. Men can explore skin treatments by following female influencers, while women can learn exercise techniques by watching male fitness YouTubers. People in their twenties can watch investment channels to start planning for retirement after hearing about the challenges facing retirees. Simultaneously, individuals in their seventies can find entertainment by viewing videos from YouTuber couples in their twenties. It is no exaggeration to say that people are now more influenced by the algorithms they encounter than by the traditional characteristics of their demographic groups, such as age, gender, or occupation.

The ease of obtaining information also indicates that individuals' abilities have expanded. With a willingness to learn, anyone can transcend boundaries of age, gender, occupation, and social status. The omnivore theory in sociology posits that as individuals accumulate cultural capital, their tastes become more open and diverse. The more knowledge one has, the greater the range of experiences one can enjoy. This principle extends beyond mere preferences; individuals who can rapidly acquire and learn information can emerge as omnivores, becoming professional creators in their teens or skilled gamers in their seventies.

Outlook & Implications

Revisiting core premises

- Question: Is TikTok really exclusive to Gen Z?
  Answer: As of the first half of 2024, 20.1% of TikTok users are over 50 years old.

- Question: Who engages more in dieting and diet management, men or women?
  Answer: According to the "Pocket CU" app from convenience store CU, the number of users subscribing to discount coupons for the "diet management" category, which includes diet substitutes like salad and chicken breast, is 1.6 times higher among men than women.

These insights reveal that actual consumer behavior often deviates from common expectations. This discrepancy highlights the risk of relying on traditional marketing strategies, which may lead to failure. In an omnivorous market where consumers defy stereotypes and curate their consumption based on personal preferences, how should companies approach segmentation and targeting strategies now?

Shifting from demographic targets to "COG"

Imagine you are marketing a refrigerator designed for newly-weds. Traditionally, you might have targeted women in their late twenties and early thirties, who are most likely to purchase wedding gifts. You would select the model favored by this demographic and advertise through channels they frequently use. This method is effective in a stable market where the product, primary customer base, and advertising channels are interconnected like a chain.

However, in the omnivore era, potential customers cannot be easily defined by demographic segments, nor can they be confined to specific channels. To effectively predict consumer behavior patterns, you must redefine your approach by incorporating new variables such as lifestyle, values, tastes, moods, and situational contexts.

To identify consumers likely to buy wedding gifts, focus on situational indicators rather than solely age. For instance, target individuals who have ordered wedding invitations, recently joined wedding preparation communities, or are searching for movers. This requires a more personalized approach, leveraging the traces left by consumers rather than broad demographic criteria.

While there may be concerns that this targeted approach will narrow your audience too much and reduce effective demand, it's crucial to understand that in an omnivore market, a narrow and precise targeting strategy is essential. Think of it not as a large hammer shattering solid ice, but rather as a sharp needle penetrating precisely where it matters.

So, what is the point of this needle? It lies in identifying the "COG" consumer. The term "COG," short for "center of gravity," originates from military strategy, initially proposed by Prussian military strategist Carl von Clausewitz. It refers to the center of power that can most effectively neutralize an adversary's capabilities. In marketing, understanding your COG consumer can help you focus your efforts on where they will have the greatest impact.

The COG concept can also be effectively applied to brands. Just as it is crucial to target the COG first in battle to achieve victory, convincing your core target – your brand's center of gravity – of the brand's value will naturally attract other potential customers.

For instance, LG Electronics reportedly favors the COG concept over traditional terms like "target" or "persona." When marketing OLED TVs, which are known for their exceptional picture quality but come with a high price tag, the company initially struggled to define its target consumers. After careful consideration, they identified gamers as the COG for this product. They specifically focused on users of "Forza Horizon," a game that, while not widely known among gamers, is particularly sensitive to picture quality. Gamers who experienced the stunning picture quality (so vivid that they can even see snowflakes while driving in the game) became enthusiastic brand advocates, generating positive word of mouth hype that significantly boosted initial marketing efforts.

In today's fast-paced society, word of mouth spreads rapidly among consumers. By effectively targeting a micro segment with a well-defined COG, even if that segment is small, brands can achieve market penetration that far surpasses traditional marketing approaches.

Post-generational humanity: Embracing perennial thinking

By 2025, South Korea is projected to enter a super-aged society, where one in five people will be over 65 years old. This demographic shift raises serious concerns, including declining productivity in the South Korean economy. It also brings challenges related to the national pension system and potential conflicts between generations. How should we respond to these challenges?

Entrepreneur Gina Pell describes this era's new image of humanity as "perennial." Originally, the term refers to plants which do not end their life cycle after blooming and bearing fruit; instead, they sprout anew with each spring. This concept suggests that we should embrace a "post-generational humanity" – one that transcends age, moving fluidly between old age and youth, much like a perennial plant. And Professor Mauro Guillén advocates for both individuals and society to break away from outdated norms, systems, and stereotypes, also adopting a perennial mindset.

The issue of the generation gap, often prevalent in organizational settings, also requires a fresh approach. While various measures, such as implementing a horizontal title system, have been attempted to address this gap, many argue that they result in superficial solutions. A survey conducted by Saramin, a career platform, found that 75.9% of 2,236 office workers felt a generation gap in the workplace. Interestingly, the most commonly cited source of this gap was between employees of the same job level (26.5%). This indicates that workplace conflicts are not merely rooted in age or job titles; rather, they reflect a broader reorganization of social norms and common sense as traditional structures of individuals, groups, and society break down.

In this new landscape, neither the market nor organizations can rely on conventional stereotypes. It is time to discard outdated beliefs and reestablish common sense. We must return to the fundamentals and rethink our assumptions.

N

Nothing Out of the Ordinary:
Very Ordinary Day

The conversation around happiness in Korean society is evolving. Rather than subscribing to the belief that "you must be happy," we propose stepping back to appreciate a life that is neither overly happy nor unhappy – one that is simply "normal, safe, and comfortable." Or, happiness that derives from, let's say, a "very ordinary day," or #VOD. In a world where each day feels like a battle, isn't it enough just to live fully in the present, even if it doesn't necessarily lead to happiness? Some may see those who embrace an ordinary day as lacking ambition or being worn out. However, these individuals are not lazy or resigned. Their commitment to living each day with intention remains unchanged. #VOD is a response to the fatigue caused by the pressure to chase "small but certain happiness," which has become performative. Isn't the obsession with pursuing and showcasing happiness itself one of the biggest obstacles to actually finding it? As socio-economic divides grow and social media increasingly promotes self-displays and conspicuousness, perhaps a routine, unadorned life is the safe space where we can breathe. Even if no remarkable happiness comes our way, today – *this* very ordinary day – matters.

#아무날

"I don't want to be too happy. Sure, I'm happy when I go on a trip or something, but eventually, I have to return to my daily routine. After experiencing happiness, the absence of it might feel even harder. It's normal that when something good happens, something bad can follow. I could get sick, something might go wrong at work, or I could have a disagreement with my family. After being happy, these challenges might feel more difficult. So, I just want tomorrow to be like today: nothing special."

– twenty-something female office worker,

from an interview with the Consumer Trend Analysis Center

How do you feel about the above statement? Do you think young people are being too mature or lacking ambition when they say, "I don't want to be too happy"? Or do you completely agree? In Korea, especially among people in their 20s and 30s, there's a noticeable shift in the conversation around happiness.

This perspective isn't just one person's isolated view – it's resonating with many. In May 2024, actor Koo Seong-hwan, better known as "Uncle Koo," appeared on the popular MBC show *I Live Alone* and became an overnight sensation. While many have appeared on the program, the response to Koo was exceptional. Why did he strike such a chord? His day-to-day life isn't filled with activities meant to impress others. He starts his morning by brushing his dog Kkotbunee꽃분이, then cooks meals from leftover ingredients, sunbathes on his rooftop, and gets chased by pigeons. He tries to maintain his image as an actor but soon gives up because it's too hard. The happiness he seeks isn't rooted in external validation. He doesn't groom his dog to make it more photogenic for others, and while he has social media, it's purely for personal use, like recording moments with his dog. He doesn't live in a fancy Seoul apartment or drive a luxury car, yet he simply states, "I'm happy because I'm me." This simple, ordinary life has unexpectedly sparked widespread admiration.

The enthusiasm for this wasn't about sharing a unique daily life on social media, gathering countless views and likes, or working tirelessly toward big or small personal goals. Nor was it about being exceptional enough to appear on TV. What truly resonated with viewers was the portrayal of a simple, relatable life – one that anyone might experience. This unexpected reaction reflects a shift in how people, especially the younger generations, are redefining happiness. The value placed on a not-so-special, ordinary day is growing, subtly but distinctly diverging from the earlier trend of "small but certain happiness소확행."

The concept of "small but certain happiness" has been a dominant trend since it was introduced in *Consumer Trend Insights 2018*. During Korea's development era, many pursued a life of sacrificing the present to prepare for a brighter future – chasing big dreams and lofty goals. For them, success equated to happiness. While this mindset led to remarkable economic growth, it also left many struggling to find personal happiness. The emergence of the small but certain happiness trend marked a shift in this thinking, suggesting that happiness isn't tied solely to winning competitions or achieving grand goals, but is instead embedded in the everyday moments of life. This idea – seeking small, tangible joys rather than striving for an uncertain, distant success – resonated deeply with many Koreans, becoming a cultural keyword that symbolized a more grounded, immediate pursuit of happiness.

From achievement-driven goals to a focus on happiness, from chasing an uncertain future to embracing the small moments of the present, Koreans' understanding of happiness has evolved significantly. One of the key changes has been an increased emphasis on quality of life. The rise of "well-being" consumption, including health care, exercise, and a stronger focus on experiences like travel and dining out, has marked this shift. It has helped temper Korea's previously showy and competitive lifestyle, encouraging people to seek personal, small certain happiness without constantly comparing themselves to others. This shift remains a positive and effective influence on daily life today.

However, at some point, the meaning of "small but certain happiness" began to shift. As the term became a popular marketing tool, it was commercialized to mean "a product or service that's slightly expensive but still within reach." For some young consumers active on social media, "#소확행" (the Korean acronym) has become synonymous with indulging in small luxuries – what they post on Instagram as "small treats." Whether it's purchasing a luxury handbag or enjoying an extravagant dessert, people readily tag these moments as "small happiness."

As the small happiness trend has spread across society, happiness has come to feel like something always within reach; albeit now, seemingly, only through public display. Whether it's a picture of running along the Han River at 5 a.m. or a snapshot from a trip abroad, simply adding the hashtag #소확행 seems to suffice. The original idea of finding joy in the little things has transformed into a social obligation: "You must be happy. If you aren't publicly recognized, are you really happy?" In the race to showcase happiness, we've come to feel the pressure of needing to share even our smallest pleasures online, turning them into items of comparison and competition. In a word, we're exhausted – not by happiness itself, but by the relentless need to perform in the competition for happiness.

As the fatigue from chasing small happiness on social media deepens, the discourse on happiness among Generation MZ is shifting. More young people are stepping away from the almost religious belief that "we must be happy." They are rejecting the idea of having their happiness evaluated by others or striving to be happy simply for show. Instead, they desire a life defined by safety and peace. When a friend asks, "How was your day?", they often reply, "It was just an ordinary day, nothing special," hoping for the reassurance that they're not living their lives wrong.

Achieving just an "ordinary day" is no small feat – it's actually something remarkable. Unimaginable disasters and accidents occur daily, often catching us off guard: cars driving the wrong way, random acts of violence from strangers, flash floods trapping people in parking lots, and sophisticated voice phishing scams draining bank accounts. These incidents make one realize that it's a blessing when nothing bad happens. I find myself grateful for the uneventful days when I can watch silly movies, collect toys, enjoy a baseball game with a beer, and simply immerse myself in daily life.

Every day is a challenge. Isn't it enough to just get through today without any problems, even if we don't reach some idealized version of happiness? It's okay not to push ourselves to feel happy all the time – surviving another day is a victory in itself. *2025 K-Consumer Trend Insights* names this emerging mindset, which values a life that is neither overly happy nor sad, but rather "normal, safe, and peaceful," as "#VOD,'" short for a "very ordinary day." In Korean, this hashtag can be written as "#aboha", or "#아보하," which is the acronym in Korean: a very ordinary day^{아주 보통의 하루}.

Various Aspects of VOD

Not a special moment, but an ordinary daily routine

"Each morning, I wake up to the familiar sound of a broom sweeping outside my window. I fold my bedding neatly, brush my teeth with care, water the plants, grab a canned coffee from the vending machine, head to work, clean the public restrooms, and enjoy a convenience store sandwich in the park." This routine repeats itself daily, yet the protagonist shows no signs of weariness.

In August 2024, Wim Wenders' *Perfect Days* surpassed 110,000 viewers within just seven weeks of its release in Korea – a remarkable achievement for an independent art film shown in a limited number of theaters, especially amid a severe economic downturn. The film's premise is simple: it follows the repetitive day-to-day life of Hirayama, a public restroom cleaner in Tokyo. His most cherished moment is capturing sunlight filtering through leaves with his film camera – a fleeting yet meaningful act. Even his seemingly mundane job of cleaning toilets is imbued with significance through the small but valuable power of routine. This portrayal of a repetitive, unremarkable life resonated with audiences, highlighting the quiet beauty in the ordinary.

#VOD emphasizes the importance of a normal, peaceful daily life. According to social analysis by Conan Technology,

mentions of words and phrases like "normal보통," "ordinary평범,"
and "without a hitch무탈" have been steadily increasing over the
past two years. What's particularly notable are the related terms
that accompany these searches: family members like "parents부
모님," "children아이," and "husband남편," ordinary meals such as
"meat and rice고기·밥," and everyday activities like "YouTube"
and "Netflix" frequently appear as key associations.

This fascination with daily life is also evident in content
creation. One standout example is the YouTube channel "Always
Recording인생 녹음중," which, since its launch in January 2024,
has amassed over 1.08 million subscribers with just 31 videos
in 8 months. What makes this channel unique is its simplicity.
The content consists of simple cartoons set to audio recordings
capturing the daily conversations of a couple at home or as they
drive – there's no overarching theme, just casual chats and playful exchanges of songs. There's no background music, just the
ambient sounds of dishes clinking or snacks being eaten.

Despite its lack of excitement, people are tuning in. The popularity of such simple, everyday content on a platform usually
filled with more stimulating material reveals a growing interest
in ordinary life. It shows that many people are seeking solace
and connection in the mundane, finding meaning in the quiet,
unspectacular moments of daily existence.

Focus on yourself, not showing off to others

The most defining characteristic of Korean consumer culture is its preoccupation with others' perceptions. This concern often drives individuals to purchase branded products, even at a higher cost, with a strong preference for luxury goods as the most extreme example. As noted earlier, there's a tendency to compare and flaunt happiness, but under the #VOD trend, the focus is shifting inward and away from showing off to others.

For instance, while buying an expensive lipstick might be viewed as a form of small but certain happiness, #VOD is more about investing in quality toothpaste instead of a luxury handbag. The use of high-quality toothpaste is a personal pleasure that remains largely invisible to others, unlike lipstick. Metaphorically, the distinction between small but certain happiness and #VOD can be likened to the difference between lipstick and toothpaste.

Interestingly, sales of premium toothpaste brands like Euthymol and Marvis have been on the rise, with Olive Young reporting a 45% increase in toothpaste sales in 2023 compared to the previous year. This trend is particularly notable considering the current climate of frugal consumption driven by the economic recession. #VOD consumption reflects a shift towards "one for me purchases나에게 집중하는 소비," emphasizing personal satisfaction and well-being rather than external validation.

In the realm of hobbies, there's a noticeable shift toward activities that bring personal joy rather than those pursued for show. Knitting, once considered a pastime primarily for grandmothers, has recently gained popularity among twenty-to-thirty-somethings. According to data from the Shinhan Card Big

Data Research Institute, the number of users frequenting "knitting specialty stores" and "knitting cafés," where patrons can enjoy a coffee while they knit, has rapidly increased in 2024 compared to 2022. Particularly noteworthy is the rising proportion of young people embracing this old hobby, which stands out in a generation typically drawn to stylish and trendy pursuits. This resurgence can be seen as an appreciation for a simple, repetitive task that enhances an ordinary day.

In the sports arena, interest is shifting away from "showy" activities like golf and tennis, which were once highly favored, towards more serious sports such as running and mountain climbing. Customer-centered data analysis platform Lotte Members looked at transaction data from January to October 2023, showing a decline in purchases of golf (-4%) and tennis (-15%) equipment and apparel, while purchases related to running (13%) and hiking (11%) have increased. Notably, the highest growth rates in sports equipment purchases were among individuals in their 20s (23%) and 30s (7%).

Golf and tennis have traditionally been associated with fashionable attire, attractive photo opportunities, and social media posts, whereas running and hiking require neither flashy gear nor ostentatious displays. They align more closely with the #VOD philosophy, allowing individuals to focus on their personal experience rather than the perceptions of others.

Recently, the practice of transcribing필사 has gained popularity in the book market. Books that encourage readers to engage

출처: 유튜브 채널 '인생 녹음 중'

- How was your day?
- Well, it was just okay. Nothing good, nothing bad.
- That's a good thing. A very ordinary day!

with meaningful sentences through handwriting are climbing the bestseller lists. This trend differs significantly from the previous calligraphy craze, which was often focused on showcasing beautiful handwriting on social media. In contrast, transcribing is a solitary activity done in the comfort of one's own room, emphasizing introspection and personal reflection. This hobby is ideal for those seeking to spend their day "hitch free무탈" while concentrating on themselves. Additionally, there has been a rapid increase in people maintaining gratitude diaries to appreciate their peaceful days. One popular method is the "Three-line Diary세줄일기," developed by the startup Willim윌림. This diary writing app allows users to record their thoughts with just one photo and three lines of text. It appeals to those who feel overwhelmed by traditional diary writing, enabling them to capture their daily experiences in a simple and manageable way.

Instead of seeking recognition from others, cultivating a positive mindset

Individuals who value an ordinary day are shifting their self-perception towards a more optimistic view, which can be described as activating their "happiness circuit." Recently, a humorous notion has emerged that suggests adopting an "idol mindset" to navigate life's challenges.

For instance, a graduate student shared that he copes with the rigors of graduate school by envisioning himself as a trainee aspiring to be an idol under the guidance of his advisor. This perspective allows him to frame his struggles as part of a journey similar to that of BlackPink's Jennie, who underwent eight years of training.

Similarly, a bank employee described how she endures the challenges of her job, where she often faces difficult customers, by imagining herself as a celebrity participating in a fan signing event. In this scenario, customers become fans waiting to engage with her one-on-one, creating a more positive narrative around her daily interactions. When confronted with particularly demanding customers, she humorously likens them to "malicious fans," which helps her manage stress.

Additionally, when a single person living alone feels reluctant to do housework, they might tell themselves, "I'm an idol on *I Live Alone*. I need to show my fans how I live, so I should clean, cook, and exercise a little." This playful reframing not only makes mundane tasks feel more meaningful but also reinforces a positive self-image.

Since early 2024, "Wonyoung-style thinking원영적 사고" has captured public interest. This trend began when Vicky Jang Wonyoung, a member of the girl group IVE, optimistically stated in a broadcast interview, "Everything that happens to me is good for me." This transcendent positivity, which reframes challenging situations as beneficial, has come to be known as "Wonyoung-style thinking."

For instance, if she finds that a bakery has run out of her favorite bread, instead of feeling disappointed, she might think,

"I'll be the first to receive freshly baked bread! I'm such a lucky Vicky!럭키비키" Similarly, there's "Heungmin-style thinking," inspired by Son Heung-min, the renowned football player known for his positive, generous outlook. This approach encourages individuals to view even negative experiences as manageable, like saying, "The bread just ran out in front of me? Just think positively, like it's still available," which is itself a take on his positive outlook when the football pitch conditions before a game are subpar – "just think they're fine!"

As these positive mindsets gained traction, new online tools emerged to facilitate this kind of thinking. One such tool is the "Wonyoung-style thinking converter원영적 사고 변환기," which transforms negative statements into upbeat affirmations. For example, if you input, "Oh, I don't want to work; the deadline is approaching," the converter would rephrase it to, "Thanks to that deadline, my skills have really improved! I'm so grateful and such a lucky Vicky!" Recently, a "Heungmin Thinking Converter" has also been introduced, further promoting this uplifting way of viewing life.

Luck, rather than happiness

"Instead of deliberately seeking happiness, I think it's nice to simply clock out of work, exercise, and enjoy a drink on the weekend without any special plans. When the weather is pleasant, it really uplifts my mood. Recently, I entered my business

card into a draw and won free extra noodles at a gamjatang
*restaurant. It may seem trivial, but it makes me feel so lucky and
genuinely happy."*

– 30-year-old office worker,

from an interview with the Consumer Trend Analysis Center

Many people express that they feel happier when good things
happen by chance. Rather than meticulously planning events,
unexpected joys often bring us greater happiness. Even within
the framework of a monotonous, ordinary day, moments of unexpected delight arise. We refer to these fortuitous occurrences
as "luck." For those who find the pursuit of happiness overwhelming, celebrating these small strokes of luck can provide
motivation and joy in their daily lives.

Moreover, there is a growing trend of actively seeking out
luck rather than passively waiting for it. This movement is not
about merely hoping for good fortune but engaging in activities
that symbolize luck. For instance, the hunt for a four-leaf clover
– a classic symbol of good luck – has become a fun and popular
pastime. Recently, cafés offering desserts and drinks shaped like
four-leaf clovers have proliferated, attracting patrons who collect
"proofies인증샷" as if stamping an attendance card. While indulging in a four-leaf clover latte or dessert won't guarantee good
fortune, it certainly offers small pleasures that bring joy.

The trend of young people seeking fortune-telling and horo-
scopes in hopes of finding a little luck in their everyday lives

is also on the rise. While one might assume that fortune-telling is primarily a pastime of older generations, it appears that individuals in their 20s are showing a heightened interest in these practices. According to an analysis by WiseApp, the number of installations for fortune-telling and astrology apps has steadily increased from 2020 to the first half of 2024. Notably, as of mid-2024, around 74.6% of users are female, and the highest usage rates are among those in their 20s, with a decline in interest noted among thirty and forty-somethings.

In line with this trend, a unique product has emerged: the "Lucky Four-Leaf Clover NFC Tag Me Lucky Keyring," created by NoPlasticSunday노플라스틱선데이. This keyring provides users with a daily fortune. By bringing the keyring close to their phones, users can access a link that prompts them to enter their name and birth date. Each time they tag the keyring, they receive their fortune for the day on their smartphone. While checking one's fortune does not guarantee positive outcomes, it reflects a growing desire among individuals to find small blessings in their daily routines, enabling them to navigate their lives with a sense of hope and positivity.

Outlook and Implications

The #VOD trend, which emphasizes finding joy in ordinary daily life and cultivating a sense of gratitude without the pressure of achieving greatness, is, however, a double-edged sword. While it promotes a healthier perspective on happiness, freeing individuals from the constant need to pursue significant achievements, it also raises concerns about the potential loss of ambition and passion among the younger generations. Parents and older generations, who sacrificed much in the pursuit of a better future, often view this trend with mixed feelings.

According to Professor Kim Young-hoon of Yonsei University, an "unrealistic positivity" that interprets reality too favorably can be just as detrimental as a negative outlook. This suggests that the #VOD movement should not be seen as a justification for complacency or a rejection of aspirations for the future. There are fears that embracing a solely present-focused mindset could lead to a state of "collective apathy," where individuals lose hope for a brighter future.

Social trends, particularly those related to life attitudes like #VOD, often mirror the socioeconomic landscape rather than reflect personal will. The trend speaks to the frustrations of young people who feel that no matter how hard they strive, they cannot achieve greater happiness. With South Korea experiencing an economic downturn and slowing growth, many find it increasingly difficult to envision a promising future. This sense of despair is particularly pronounced among the younger generations. A report by the Korea Institute for Health and Social Affairs revealed that individuals born between 1986 and 2001 perceive a lack of hope for the future, with concerns about ongoing employment challenges and difficulty adapting to rapid changes in society. In light of these pressures, it is understandable that many young people shift their focus to finding comfort and contentment in their current lives.

The #VOD trend offers a potential path to healing in a society overwhelmed by feelings of depression and despair. In a world that often pressures individuals to consume more and to succeed at all costs, the focus on finding contentment in everyday life can serve as a refreshing alternative. As public speaker and journalist Jennifer Moss eloquently states, "we're not happy when we're chasing happiness. We're happiest when we're not thinking about it, when we're enjoying the present moment because we're lost in a meaningful project, working toward a higher goal, or helping someone who needs us." (Happiness Isn't the Absence of Negative Feelings / Harvard Business Review, 2015.8.20.)

For those who have experienced illness, the value of simple routines becomes clear. The ability to perform everyday tasks – like scratching an itch or enjoying a warm bath – often highlights the blessings of life that are taken for granted. In moments of discomfort, aspirations for success and happiness feel distant, underscoring the idea that true contentment is often rooted in the absence of pain or struggle. This parallels the notion that individuals who genuinely experience satisfaction do not obsess over happiness; rather, those who chase it are often acknowledging their current lack of fulfillment.

The concept of the "Goldilocks principle" further illustrates this perspective. Just as our planet thrives in a balanced environment, happiness may also lie in moderation – embracing a life that is neither excessively joyful nor overly discontented. This balanced approach to life allows for the appreciation of ordinary moments as the foundation for a fulfilling existence, even for those who strive for remarkable achievements.

In a competitive society where many feel compelled to chase extraordinary accomplishments, it is vital to recognize the significance of ordinary days. These moments, while seemingly unremarkable, are essential for building a sense of well-being. The #VOD philosophy encourages individuals to find value in the mundane, reminding us that today's simple experiences can provide a sense of peace and contentment, regardless of the pursuit of capital-H "Happiness." Ultimately, even without extraordinary moments, the importance of living a very ordinary day should not be underestimated.

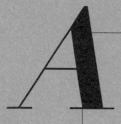

All About
the Toppings

트립영경제

"I don't like things that are the same as everyone else's." Just like adding toppings on pizza, more consumers today are customizing ready-made products to reflect their individuality. Personalizing items to stand out isn't new, but now consumers are choosing more unique and diverse options – even when the extras cost more than the base product. This shift, where secondary elements or "toppings" become the focus and drive new economic trends, is called the "toppings economy."

People are more passionate about decorating than ever. They put patches of their favorite characters on their T-shirts and attach multiple keychains to their bags. They also tend to seek the "perfect fit" for themselves rather than simply the "best" product. Consumers create their own ideal combinations by mixing elements offered by manufacturers.

The rise of the toppings economy signals that today's market is about giving consumers the power to express individuality and creativity. Instead of offering a perfectly finished product, companies should focus on creating a flexible ecosystem where customers can engage, reinterpret, and personalize. After all, a product isn't complete until the customer adds their toppings.

*#1. "I often bump into people wearing the same sneakers, and it makes me a bit uncomfortable. That's when I started 'shinkku*신꾸*' (decorating shoes) after seeing it on Instagram."*

*#2. "My go-to drink these days is 'amangchu*아망추*.' It's iced tea with frozen mango chunks instead of ice, and it's a perfect match for my taste!"*

People dislike sameness. They seek out products that reflect their individuality. A new generation has emerged, following their mantra: "there's no other product like this in the world." They're tired of perfect products and prefer items that feel unfinished until they've put their own spin on them. They favor products with the potential for personalization over mass-produced, factory-made goods. The number of people who express their uniqueness through consumption is steadily growing.

As more consumers seek the "perfect fit" that aligns with their personal tastes, rather than the accepted "best" product, industries are shifting to accommodate. Companies are now offering products with room for personalization instead of fully finished items. As a result, additional, customizable features are gaining more value than the core aspects of the product, forming a market where the extras matter more than the basics.

Additional decorations or options added to a basic product are often referred to as "toppings." Pizza is the prime example – various toppings are added to a simple dough base to create the perfect flavor for each individual. While customers may have not felt so strongly about toppings in the past, they are now central to crafting one's personal favorite item. In recognition of this shift, *2025 K-Consumer Trend Insights* has coined the term "toppings economy" to describe how these secondary elements are gaining more attention and having a new economic impact. Toppings, which allow consumers to use products in flexible, personalized ways, are now crucial for enhancing customer satisfaction.

Personalizing mass-produced products isn't new, but the toppings economy is expanding across industries like fashion and food, as detailed below. This trend goes beyond traditional customization by anticipating post-purchase modifications and catering to even the smallest differences among a wide range of options.

Three Types of Toppings Economy

1. Maximized decoration: Toppings upon toppings

The first type of toppings economy is the "*kku-kku-kku꾸꾸꾸*"

trend, which revolves around the concept of endlessly decorating (*kkumida*꾸미다) items with multiple layers of toppings. This is a shift from the previous "*kku-an-kku*꾸안꾸" trend, which focused on subtle decoration that appeared effortless ("*kku-an-kku*" literally means "decorated, but not decorated"). Now, the trend has evolved into fully embracing decoration, which is referred to as "*kku-kku-kku*," meaning triple decoration in Korean. People add *wappens*와펜 (cloth patches, from the German for "coat of arms") of their favorite characters on T-shirts, and attach multiple key rings to their bags. Rather than using products as-is, they apply various decorative toppings to create something uniquely their own.

In the past, decoration trends were mainly limited to specific items like "*phon-kku*" (phone decorations) or "*da-kku*" (diary decorations) among the younger generations. However, this trend is now expanding to nearly all types of products. Data from Conan Technology shows a rising number of mentions of decoration-related keywords over the last two years. What's notable is the growing variety of decoration topics. Beyond traditional items like mobile phones and cakes, people are now customizing everyday products such as eco-bags, suitcases, handbags ("*baeg-kku*"), indoor shoes and sneakers ("*shin-kku*"), as well as T-shirts and keyboards. This marks the arrival of a true "anything-*kku*" era, where individuals freely decorate any product to match their personal style, without limitations.

The decoration craze has recently swept through the fashion industry as well, with products and services designed to leave room for personalization popping up one after another. For example, Gentle Monster caused a stir by collaborating with Blackpink's Jennie to release sunglasses that allow users to attach various charms. The charms ranged from pearls and ribbons to cute animal figures, turning sunglasses into customizable accessories. The product became a sensation on social media, sparking a trend of "sunglasses decoration선꾸." Even luxury brands are embracing this movement. For the 2024 Spring/Summer season, Miu Miu introduced a line of bag decoration items, featuring keychains, leather key rings, and mini pouches that could be attached to bags. These bag accessories were organized into a separate category on the official Miu Miu website, signaling the rise of a new product segment.

In this environment, pop-up stores and small shops specializing in small-size decorative accessories, particularly popular among teens and twenty-somethings, are also thriving. One example is Object Sangga옵젳상가 in Mapo-gu, Seoul. The store offers customers a wide selection of pouches and bags in various colors, along with toppings like *wappens* and key rings, so they can create personalized items. Its appeal lies in the fun of decorating, and its popularity has spread by word of mouth. The shop has recently expanded its presence by opening a store in Muji and supporting collaborations with brands like Ottogi. Similarly, Dongdaemun Market has emerged as a hotspot, attracting the younger generations who visit accessory supply stores to buy decorative materials, as many such stores are concentrated in the area.

Some people are even putting stickers on their faces as part of their personal styling, a trend known as "*eol-kku*얼꾸" (face decoration). This trend, which began with overseas celebrities, involves decorating the face with cute acne patches shaped like stars or hearts to cover blemishes that were difficult to hide. Recently, local celebrities have also embraced this style, using various patch stickers in different shapes. As a result, numerous brands are launching adorable *eol-kku* stickers, and the trend is spreading as a fun, alternative way to finish off a makeup look.

The decoration craze fueled by toppings has also taken over social platforms. On Instagram, "Story decoration" has become popular. When users post a Story with a good photo, they can add a variety of stickers to the image, similar to how people decorate diaries. Stickers have become so important that entire Instagram accounts are dedicated to curating and sharing the best stickers for story decoration. Some people even go a step further by removing the background from their own images to create personalized stickers.

2. "Optimal" rather than "best"; Toppings just for me

"I'm 22.5C1!"

This is the exclamation of a consumer who has discovered a cosmetic shade that perfectly complements her skin tone. Why

22.5, instead of 21 or 23? Consumers who struggle to find the right products are known as "___ nomads." For instance, those unable to locate a matching foundation shade are referred to as "foundation nomads." Traditionally, domestic beauty brands have primarily offered foundation colors by differences of two, e.g., 19, 21, and 23, but recently, 1:1 customized products powered by AI have emerged, transforming foundation nomads into loyal brand residents. Amorepacific's "Tonework" is a foundation that breaks down skin brightness into 0.5 increments and categorizes skin tones into five types, like C2, C1, and N, resulting in a total of 205 shades, which is a game-changer for foundation nomads. AI analyzes individual skin tones to guide customers in finding their perfect match. And there's more: the newly launched "DukheeRx덕히알엑스" utilizes AI to instantly assess skin conditions through a smartphone photo, offering tailored skincare solutions from a database of 48,000 options.

In this context, the second type of toppings economy is a movement aimed at seeking the "optimal" product tailored to individual needs rather than the "best" product for the masses. Consequently, companies are creating products and services that allow for a wide range of combinations with numerous toppings, emphasizing personalized experiences. This aligns closely with the concept of customization. While DIY, customization, and personalized products have existed before, the toppings economy has evolved to facilitate precise individual optimization that accounts for even the smallest differences.

In many industries, it has become common to offer a wide range of combinations, with the message, "I don't know what you'll like, so I prepared a bit of everything." A notable example is Dyson, which recently made waves by announcing its Bluetooth headphones, the Dyson OnTrac, set to launch this year. Known primarily for its vacuum cleaners and hair dryers, Dyson's entry into the audio equipment market has garnered significant attention, particularly with its 2,000+ customization options available. Consumers can choose not only the headband color but also various styles and finishes for the ear cushions and ear cups, allowing for truly personalized headphones that fit individual preferences.

Similarly, the fashion industry is expanding custom-made services using various technologies. For instance, Fila offers a tennis shoe customization service that considers individual tastes and foot shapes. Customers can select their desired shoe model, choose the fit that suits their feet, and even specify the type of tennis court they frequently play on. Additionally, they can mix and match colors for the front, sides, shoelaces, and soles, resulting in a pair of tennis shoes that reflect their unique style.

Meanwhile, eyewear brand Breezm브리즘 provides one-on-one consultations lasting about an hour to help customers find the best glasses for their needs. Utilizing 3D scanning and printing, they assess various factors such as face shape, eyebrow width, nose height, and ear positioning to create customized glasses tailored to each individual's features, offering 650,000 possible combinations. Their services have received a warm response in Korea and they have recently expanded into the U.S. market.

Adding new toppings to beverages has become a trendy way to discover your own "best combination." Consequently, the blending beverage market, which mixes different drinks to create new flavors or aromas, is on the rise. Recently, various blending recipes have gained popularity on social media, including "*ashotchu*" (iced tea with an espresso shot), "*oshotchu*" (orange juice with an espresso shot), "*leshotchu*" (lemonade with an espresso shot), "*sashotchu*" ("cider," or lemon-flavored soda, with an espresso shot), and "*amangchu*" (iced tea with frozen mango added).

3. "Transformation" rather than "completion": Modular toppings that can be changed at any time

The final aspect of the toppings economy trend is the use of modular toppings that can be easily added or removed to transform products on the go. Nowadays, consumers prefer to keep the option for continuous change open even after a purchase. For instance, a single smartwatch can be paired with various straps that users can switch out to enhance functionality. They might opt for a sports strap for gym workouts, which is easy to clean, or a leather strap for an important dinner. This approach allows for changes depending on your mood and without the financial burden, as the straps are generally more affordable than the watch itself. To facilitate this, dedicated pouches capable of holding over ten colorful straps have emerged, making it feel like users own multiple watches with just a quick swap.

The "modular design" trend that is spreading across various industries aligns with this concept. It allows products to be expanded based on consumer needs or preferences by combining or replacing different modular components, much like Lego blocks. A notable example is the enduring popularity of "modular sofas," which enable consumers to arrange their spaces as desired by mixing and matching various units. On social media, you can find review videos of individuals rearranging their sofas into ㄱ, ㅡ, or ㄷ shapes depending on their mood or the situation, or transforming their setup by adding additional units.

Modular design is increasingly making its way into the entire furniture market. The "Cusino Cozy" by Ilum일룸 is gaining traction as a versatile bed that adapts to consumers' life stages. Initially designed as a bed for newlyweds, it can later accommodate a growing family by adding a single bed that attaches to the side. With additional options like bed guards and footboards, it easily transforms into a secure family bed.

Office environment specialist brand Fursys퍼시스 has introduced the "Aerie Module" series, which can be reconfigured based on the size of the space or the number of users. Depending on how the modules are combined, the furniture can create a variety of layouts, including straight lines, corners, semicircles, S-shapes, T-shapes, and X-shapes. The series has received prestigious recognition, winning the Red Dot design award in Germany and the IDEA award in the U.S. It is garnering attention for its

- Decorate, decorate, and decorate again.
- Nothing under the sky is the same.
- Leave me room to decorate. Perfection is boring.

support of a hybrid work environment that facilitates meetings, work tasks, and relaxation, moving away from traditional workspace designs.

Modular design is set to extend to automobiles as well. Similar to how you can rearrange furniture in your home, car interiors will soon allow individuals to add or remove specific functions based on their preferences. In January 2024, Kia announced a shift in its business model by redefining the PBV (Purpose Built Vehicle) concept to "Platform Beyond Vehicle." This innovative approach aims to provide consumers with a flexible experience, enabling them to modify the interior space by swapping out vehicle bodies according to their intended use. The PBV will allow customers to select configurations tailored to their needs, with options for various body types, including basic, delivery, and chassis cab. The first mass production is scheduled for July 2025.

Even apartments can now be easily transformed like Legos. Moving away from fixed, uniform floor plans, a new concept is emerging that allows residents to adapt their living spaces to suit their lifestyles. In August 2024, POSCO E&C launched the "Flexi-form" floor plan, which emphasizes customizability. This design enables individuals to separate the sleeping area in the master bedroom based on their sleeping patterns by installing a door or creating an additional living space within the bedroom. Notably, the pillars in these apartments are positioned on the exterior to minimize load-bearing walls, allowing residents to modify their spaces as desired.

Similarly, Samsung C&T's apartment brand Raemian래미안 has introduced "The Next Home," a futuristic housing model that grants residents the freedom to transform their living environments according to their needs. This model not only allows for flexible interior changes but also incorporates pre-fabricated modules that can be easily inserted, enabling a transformation reminiscent of assembling Lego pieces.

The Significance and Background of the Toppings Economy

"What is your favorite topping?"

In the first half of this year, the most popular domestic dessert franchise was "Yoajung요아정" (short for "yogurt ice cream's요아" "essence정수"). According to Shinhan Card's Big Data Analysis Center, Yoajung's usage surged by approximately 422% compared to the same period last year. While "Dubai Chocolate" was another trendy item, what was it that made yogurt ice cream, which isn't particularly new, stand out? The answer lies in the toppings, not the ice cream itself, which became the star of the product. With over 50 types of toppings available, consumers were able to craft their own unique combinations, and the trend quickly spread as people shared their favorite combinations. One combination, recommended by a male idol, became a sensation and was jokingly called the "500 million won" due to the extravagant number of toppings added.

The emergence of the toppings economy is rooted in a historical context that transcends mere short-term tactics or marketing strategies aimed at creating popular products. To understand this phenomenon, we can explore its background through two key dimensions: shifts in industrial paradigms and changes in consumer preferences.

Industrial significance: From standardized economy to toppings economy

If one event could be identified as the catalyst for the most significant change in human consumption, it would be the advent of Fordism. On April 1, 1913, Henry Ford introduced the first conveyor belt system at an automobile factory in Michigan. This large-scale conveyor belt maximized productivity by standardizing the production process, marking the dawn of Fordism, a hallmark of the mass production system. Fordism dramatically enhanced production efficiency, moving beyond home-based handicrafts and ushering in the "age of abundance" by alleviating chronic supply shortages. This approach soon spread across industries, becoming the cornerstone of commodity capitalism's market economy.

Fordism was characterized by a focus on standardization, prioritizing the universal needs of the public over the specific needs of individual consumers. It aimed to maximize efficiency through mass production based on standardized criteria, emphasizing product homogeneity while viewing non-homogeneous products as defective. In this standardized economy, consumers simply purchased products, with little room for customization or additional engagement.

Fast forward more than a century, and as product quality has reached a high level of standardization, consumers are increasingly losing interest in generic, one-size-fits-all products. The rise of consumers seeking unique and distinctive items has sparked a transition from the standardized economy, where product homogeneity was paramount, to the toppings economy. This shift reflects a growing desire for personalized experiences and products. Meanwhile, advancements in various technologies have enabled personalized product production, which was previously hindered by profitability concerns, to become a viable reality.

As generative AI technology continues to advance, it is paving the way for an almost infinite toppings economy. A prime example is Krafton's new game, "inZOI인조이", which has garnered attention for its revolutionary character customization features. In this life simulation game, users take on the role of gods, creating their desired life and exploring various narratives. The game has drawn global interest due to its highly detailed customization options available during the character creation process. Players can modify everything from hairstyles and facial features to body shapes, shirt sleeve lengths, and nail designs. Moreover, players can utilize prompt-based image-generating AI to create countless designs for various objects, including clothing and furniture. After its launch, inZOI generated over 100,000 unique creations in just two days, with some characters resembling real people, including famous girl group idols and U.S. presidents, sparking significant buzz.

This technological advancement enhances the efficiency of customized production and facilitates hyper-personalization, aligning perfectly with consumers' desires for their own unique creations. As a result, this evolution into the toppings economy is accelerating, reflecting a growing trend toward individualized experiences and products.

Changes in consumers: From purchase satisfaction to efficacy

The second critical factor to consider is the evolving nature of consumers. Consumption has traditionally been a balancing act between belonging and differentiation. On one hand, there is a strong desire for belonging – wanting to possess what others have – but on the other, there is a compelling urge for differentiation, to stand out from the crowd. As personal tastes evolve from simple preferences to competitive advantages, the inclination to seek unique experiences in consumption has intensified.

Today's consumers are increasingly sensitive to trends and often engage in conformity consumption, yet they shy away from being completely identical to others. For instance, when everyone wears the same trendy outfit, it becomes known as a "clone look," and contemporary consumers actively avoid this phenomenon because who wants to be a clone?

Particularly influential in this shift is Gen Z, born between 1995 and 2009, which is rapidly emerging as a formidable consumer force. This generation goes beyond merely seeking personalization; they favor "creative consumption" that allows them to proactively customize and modify their preferences. Popular food items like *malatang*, bubble tea, and yogurt illustrate this trend, as each consumer can select their favorite toppings to curate their own unique experience. This approach to topping consumption is not limited to food; it is now permeating various sectors, including fashion, beauty, interior design, construction, and finance, further solidifying the rise of the toppings economy.

Outlook & Implications

The success of the toppings economy highlights the importance of addressing consumer preferences and behaviors in product development. To create successful toppings that resonate with consumers, several key considerations should be taken into account.

Don't forget the "dough"

While focusing on toppings is essential, it's crucial not to over-look the foundational elements of a product. Emphasizing only the additional features can lead to neglecting the core aspects that define its quality and functionality. Just as the dough is vital for a delicious pizza, the basic functions, quality, and integrity of a product must be prioritized for the toppings to hold any signifi-cance.

Take for instance Google's modular smartphone project, "Project Ara." Launched with the promise of revolutionizing the smartphone market through modular components that allowed consumers to customize their devices, the project was ultimately suspended in September 2016 after three years of development. While the concept had advantages – enabling users to select only the features they want and upgrade parts as needed – the project faced challenges in achieving essential smartphone values like durability and price competitiveness. The failure to balance inno-vative toppings with these fundamental elements contributed to its demise.

Conversely, Samsung Electronics successfully introduced the "Music Frame", a customizable frame-type speaker. This product garnered positive reviews not only for its ability to serve as an art piece by displaying desired photos and decorative panels but also for excelling in its primary function: sound quality. The Music Frame features six speakers designed for high, mid, low, and vibrational frequencies within a compact design. Its AI technology optimizes sound based on the room's acoustics and automatically adjusts equalization for various content genres, such as music, movies, and games.

This example illustrates that for a product to be truly meaningful and successful, it must effectively balance both the "basics" and the "toppings."

Creating a toppings ecosystem that strengthens relationships with customers

Once the foundational elements of the topping economy are in place, the ultimate goal is to establish a "toppings ecosystem" that allows for continuous addition and innovation of toppings. This means developing a system that can create ongoing added value, rather than merely offering one-off toppings.

A prime example is Starbucks, which provides a custom order service enabling customers to personalize their drinks by adding or removing syrup, milk, and Java chips, among many other toppings. Theoretically, this service can yield an astounding 388 billion possible latte combinations. However, this customization poses challenges, complicating menu creation and increasing the workload for baristas, which has led to tensions between management and employees. To address this, Starbucks plans to invest up to $3 billion annually by 2025 in automated equipment designed to simplify the preparation of customized drinks, helping baristas manage the complex orders without needing to memorize each customer's preferences.

While Starbucks' custom menu may appear to be a financial burden due to the associated costs, it has also become a significant driver of sales. According to 2023 sales data, customized drinks accounted for 76% of total sales in the US. Furthermore, young consumers frequently share photos of their unique creations on social media, promoting their personalized drinks and contributing to the brand's visibility.

Establishing a system that fosters a thriving topping economy can cultivate a direct and meaningful relationship between customers and companies. By encouraging customer participation, despite the initial costs, brands can enhance loyalty and engagement, ultimately driving sales and creating a vibrant community around their products.

Crocs serves as another prime example of creating an ecosystem centered around toppings. Once labeled one of the "50 Worst Inventions" by *Time* magazine in 2010, Crocs has now risen to become one of the most popular fashion brands in the world, selling an impressive 150 million pairs annually. A significant factor in this resurgence is their accessories known as "Jibbitz," which fit into the shoe's holes, enabling near-infinite customization. The ability to transform the look of the shoes simply by changing the Jibbitz has contributed greatly to Crocs' appeal.

In South Korea, Crocs continue to enjoy strong popularity; sales from January to April 2024 increased by 30% year-on-year, maintaining the same growth trend as the previous year. The brand is also experiencing explosive growth in China, with a reported triple-digit increase in sales in the first quarter of 2024 alone.

This illustrates how a toppings ecosystem can maximize engagement by encouraging customers to not just buy a product, but to continuously explore and interact with the brand even after their initial purchase. Companies must create opportunities for consumers to reinterpret and actively participate in their products by developing diverse toppings ecosystems.

After all, a product is only truly complete when the customer adds their personal touch with toppings.

K

Keeping it Human:
Face Tech

First impressions matter to everyone, which is why we invest in our appearances. The same principle applies to technology. 'Face tech,' a breakthrough that adds expressions to machines, accurately reads and interprets human faces and emotions, creating personalized faces for each user. This technology is becoming increasingly vital as it enhances user experience by offering clear instructions and minimizing cognitive errors when interacting with complex devices. It also fosters a sense of familiarity. Today, people evaluate a robot's effectiveness based on its human-like qualities rather than the sophistication of its AI.

While user interface (UI) has been important, the focus is shifting towards affordance—the ease of recognizing and using something intuitively without prior instruction. Face tech excels in providing the most intuitive and effortless affordance.

In the age of generative AI, companies and products that engage with users in a 'human-like' manner, understanding and responding to emotions, will stand out. Amidst a competitive landscape brimming with new technologies, Face tech offers a significant edge by bringing technology closer to human interaction.

페이스테크

In 2014, when the city of Seoul introduced bus headlights designed to resemble eyes, children were thrilled. Parents, however, found themselves in a dilemma, as their kids eagerly demanded bus rides, mistaking the buses for the beloved animation character from *Tayo the Little Bus*꼬마버스 타요. Fast forward 11 years, and it's not just buses in Seoul sporting these eye designs – trucks and various other vehicles are adorned with them too. Moreover, this trend has expanded beyond vehicles; delivery robots in restaurants and guide robots at airports now assist people with amusing facial expressions.

This phenomenon reflects a burgeoning trend known as "face tech," where technology increasingly mimics, interprets, and generates human-like faces and expressions. In an era marked by rapid technological advancements, faces have become crucial because they offer an intuitive entry point for users encountering new and complex technologies. By reducing cognitive errors and encouraging familiarity, these human-like features make technology more accessible. Today, consumers evaluate the effectiveness of robots not just by the sophistication of their AI, but by how closely they resemble human beings in their expressions and interactions.

It's widely understood that first impressions are formed within just three seconds when people meet. The same principle applies to technology. When we perceive a human-like expression on an otherwise lifeless object, it naturally grabs our attention. In fact, when a new product concept enters the market, the expression it conveys in those initial moments can be a decisive factor in its success or failure. This is especially true now, as we emerge from a period when masks during the COVID-19 pandemic obscured our faces and expressions, making them an even more valuable commodity. So, take a moment to consider: What kind of expressions are your products – or you yourself – presenting to your customers?

Three Types of Face Tech

The most famous face in the world is probably that of the *Mona Lisa*, housed in the Louvre Museum in Paris. The *Mona Lisa*, which is uniquely eyebrow-less, is one of the most visited works of art in the world, with an average of 20,000 to 30,000 people locking eyes with her every day. Another iconic artwork known for its expression is Edvard Munch's *The Scream*. The expressionist masterpiece captures distorted facial expressions that vividly convey deep-seated emotions such as anxiety, fear, and despair, evoking powerful reactions from those who view it.

While "face" and "expression" are closely related, there are differences. The face refers to the front part of the head, where features like the eyes, nose, mouth, forehead, and chin are located. It serves as a canvas for displaying emotions through the delicate movements of various muscles, i.e., expressions. Because each person's face is unique, it plays a crucial role in identifying individuals, while expressions are vital in nonverbal communication, conveying emotions and mental states that are mostly universal. Interestingly, the English word "face" can refer to both the physical face and its expressions, which is why the term "face tech" should be understood to encompasses both aspects.

1. Adding expressions to technology

There is a growing effort to bring liveliness and a sense of friendliness to technology by embedding human expressions into inanimate objects, such as machines. Electric vehicles, unlike those with internal combustion engines, don't require front grilles, offering designers more creative freedom. This has led to the development of "grille displays," where LED screens are placed on the front of vehicles – essentially their faces – to display human-like expressions. These LED displays allow vehicles to convey emotions and intentions to other drivers and pedestrians. For instance, a vehicle might display a smiling face to signal a pedestrian that it's safe to cross the street, or it could greet a driver with a welcoming expression as they approach. Such interactions help make the relationship between vehicles and users more human and engaging.

Similarly, "lamp language" is a feature that allows vehicles to express a range of emotions and intentions through their headlamps and rear lamps. Electric vehicles, which rely on electricity to control various lights, can create more complex and nuanced expressions. By manipulating the color, brightness, and blinking patterns of LED lamps, vehicles can communicate different messages to drivers and pedestrians. For example, when the vehicle comes to a stop, the headlamps might blink softly to convey gratitude, or when parking, the rear lamps could shine brightly to guide the driver to a parking space. This makes interactions between vehicles and people more intuitive and emotionally resonant.

In January 2024, the home robot market, previously overlooked at the US Consumer Electronics Show (CES), suddenly gained significant attention. A standout was LG Electronics' introduction of the "Smart Home AI Agent, Q9," which captivated attendees with its adorable expressions. While this device was showcased as a "mobile home hub," featuring advanced technology that allows it to move upright on two wheels – a challenging feat in robotics – what truly won people over was its charming face with round, heart-shaped eyes, earning it the reputation of a "companion robot." During its development, great care was taken to humanize the mobile AI home hub, equipping it with a 7-inch display for the face and crafting over 43 delicate eye shapes to create various expressions. The result was a crowd-pleaser, with visitors cheering as this robot, donning large headphones, smoothly rolled around the exhibition hall on two wheels.

Looking ahead, regardless of their functions, the facial expressions of robot devices entering our homes are likely to provide a critical competitive edge. Even the most advanced generative AI won't seamlessly integrate into consumers' daily lives if it is seen as unapproachable or complex. In the future, consumer electronics products will need to be designed to engage with users in a friendly and accessible manner.

Even AI chatbots, which lack physical form, are rapidly evolving into digital humans capable of making facial expressions. These digital humans offer more natural and immersive interactions, significantly enhancing user experience, making them highly valuable in customer service and support roles. They operate 24 hours a day and are highly efficient, effortlessly communicating in multiple languages. At NVIDIA's annual developer conference, GTC 2024, AI communication company Cleon클레온 showcased its cutting-edge AI digital human technology, which can converse and express itself with a wide range of emotions in real-time, much like a human. Cleon's innovative technology allows for the creation of digital humans using just a single photo and 30 seconds of voice data, enabling them to convey various emotions and engage in human-like conversations. The technology emphasizes the importance of natural facial expressions and movements, driven by emotional data, positioning Cleon at the forefront of digital human advancements. They achieved these nuanced emotional expressions by leveraging NVIDIA's A2F (Audio2Face) application.

2. Interpreting facial expressions

In Pixar's animation *Inside Out 2*, the main character, Riley, discovers that her friends have transferred to different schools by observing their subtle facial expressions. She pays close attention to their eyebrows, quickly realizing something is amiss by analyzing their movements, the depth of wrinkles, and the extent of frowning or squinting.

The ability to read facial expressions is crucial not only in films but also in our daily lives. Charles Darwin highlighted the significant role that facial expressions play in human evolution. By interpreting emotional signals like fear, anger, and danger in the expressions of others and responding appropriately, individuals were better equipped for survival.

Now, technology is beginning to develop the ability to read human faces and expressions, a capability that can be broadly categorized into two main areas: (1) recognizing individual faces for identity verification, and (2) interpreting unique emotional expressions that are difficult to convey in words to better understand a user's state.

The first category is exemplified by smartphones and door locks that utilize facial recognition for authentication. This technology has been around for some time but continues to evolve rapidly. The facial recognition market is projected to grow at a compound annual growth rate of 16.13% from 2023 to 2030, nearly three times the expected growth rate of the fingerprint recognition market during the same period.

One notable player in this field is FaceMe, a facial recognition technology company founded by Taiwan's CyberLink. Their technology has garnered attention for its digital forgery prevention capabilities, allowing it to determine when a photo does not represent a real face. This feature is crucial for smart door locks that can unlock various types of locks. Additionally, major tech companies are also offering facial analysis technologies, such as Microsoft's Azure Face API and Amazon's Rekognition, further advancing the capabilities of facial recognition in various applications.

China is at the forefront of facial recognition technology, largely due to fewer regulations surrounding personal biometric data. One of the innovations emerging from this landscape is a payment system that utilizes facial recognition. Alipay has introduced a feature called "Smile-to-Pay" (now updated and dubbed "Dragonfly"), which allows users to complete transactions simply by looking at a screen and smiling. Similarly, Tencent has developed a program called "Frog Pro," which enables facial recognition payments through WeChat, allowing users to make payments without even needing a smartphone.

In the financial sector, Shinhan Card became the first company to implement a non-face-to-face real-name authentication service using facial recognition. This streamlined system verifies identity through real-time facial images when applying for a card via a mobile application. Users can select facial authentication during the application process and immediately authenticate themselves using just a facial image captured by their phone camera, requiring no additional setup.

Beyond simple authentication, technology is evolving to recognize and interpret emotions through facial expressions and respond appropriately. For instance, Hyundai Motor Company's children's mobility initiative, "Little Big Emotion," utilizes Emotion Adaptive Vehicle Control (EAVC) technology, facilitating communication between the vehicle and its passengers. This is particularly crucial in the future of autonomous driving, especially for hospitalized children who often perceive the short distance from their hospital room to the examination room as a daunting journey. Currently being piloted at the SJD Barcelona Children's Hospital in Spain, this technology features emotion-responsive ambient lighting at the bottom of the vehicle, which changes color based on the child's emotional state. Red indicates high fear, yellow suggests reduced anxiety, and green signals readiness for treatment. Additionally, the vehicle's front display plays various animations and music that correspond with the EAVC system, enhancing the overall experience for young patients.

Reading facial expressions in the medical field has proven to be incredibly valuable, with emotion recognition technology that combines artificial intelligence and healthcare emerging as a transformative tool for enhancing patient treatment and well-being. Japanese IT company NEC has developed advanced facial recognition technology capable of detecting users' facial patterns and pupil conditions, as well as analyzing patients' subtle expressions, voice intonation, and other signals through a mobile device. This technology can estimate an individual's biological and mental state by carefully analyzing these indicators, allowing for the identification of subtle nonverbal cues that can provide insights into a patient's health. Consequently, AI-driven emotion recognition offers medical professionals unprecedented insight into patients' emotional states, surpassing traditional diagnostic methods and paving the way for a truly hyper-personalized treatment experience.

In the automotive sector, driver expression monitoring systems play a crucial role in enhancing safety by detecting drowsiness and distraction. The Driver Monitoring System of Australia-based safety tech company Seeing Machines tracks the driver's eyes and facial expressions in real time, issuing warnings and, if necessary, interfacing with the vehicle control system to help prevent accidents. Bosch employs in-vehicle cameras and AI algorithms to monitor and analyze drivers' blinking, gaze direction, and facial angles instantaneously. Similarly, Nissan's ProPILOT 2.0 system utilizes facial recognition technology to assess driver attention, providing alerts if the driver is distracted and linking to driving assistance functions to enhance safety. Tesla has recently announced plans to incorporate facial recognition with its in-vehicle camera system, allowing for personalized settings based on the driver. This system could even call 911 if the driver fails to respond, or autonomously navigate to the nearest hospital if the driver is incapacitated.

3. Creating your own expressions

Genmoji, a new feature introduced in iOS following the announcement of Apple Intelligence, sets itself apart from traditional emojis. Similar to ChatGPT, users can describe their desired emoji in a text field, and AI will generate several new emojis based on that description. Users can then select their favorite to use. The name "Genmoji," a blend of "generate" and "emoji," represents one of the innovative AI features set to be rolled out for Apple devices by the end of 2024. Additionally, Moji Maker from AppMoji, Inc. offers users the ability to create personalized emojis, allowing for the design of customized emojis that reflect individual expressions and moods, thereby diversifying digital communication. This capability of creating personalized expressions for non-face-to-face interactions falls under the emerging domain of "creating your own expressions" within face tech.

The beauty industry is at the forefront of developing technologies for facial expression creation. In his keynote address at CES 2024, L'Oréal CEO Nicolas Hieronymus emphasized the company's commitment to blending beauty and technology, saying that the company is trying to create beauty products based on technology, not technology products based on beauty. Numerous beauty brands are competing to innovate in the realm of "creating unique facial expressions" through beauty tech. For instance, L'Oréal's ModiFace allows users to see how makeup products will appear on their faces in real-time via its virtual makeup try-on feature. This enables users to experiment with various lipstick and eyeshadow colors using their smartphone cameras, facilitating safe online purchases without the need for in-person trials.

Several beauty brands, including Estée Lauder, Aveda, and Benefit Cosmetics, have reported positive outcomes from their virtual try-on tools that utilize AI and AR technologies. Estée Lauder experienced increased customer loyalty thanks to its AI-driven iMatch™ Virtual Shade Expert tool, which also led to a 2.5-fold rise in conversions for virtual try-ons of lipsticks. Aveda reported a 220% increase in traffic to its virtual try-on tool and a 14% boost in sales from users of the feature. Furthermore, Benefit Cosmetics saw a 300% increase in conversions and a 10% rise in average order value after launching the NARS Matchmaker tool. These impressive metrics, highlighting improved conversions and larger shopping carts, clearly illustrate the connection between beauty tech that enables self-expression and face tech. Amorepacific is also enhancing its brand presence by launching a Laneige Instagram filter targeting Japan's Gen MZ demographic, incorporating their new product, the "Bouncy Sleeping Mask," into a Korean-style four-cut instant photo filter frame to capture the essence and emotions of K-Pop culture.

Why Are Facial Expressions Important?

Facial expressions serve as the most fundamental means of communication

The face is intricately tied to human identity, with expressions transcending language barriers. Charles Darwin, in *The Expression of the Emotions in Man and Animals*, suggested that facial expressions are evolutionary responses to environmental challenges, sharing commonalities with those of animals. From an evolutionary standpoint, these expressions are adaptive mechanisms essential for survival, facilitating communication and social interaction.

Long before language was developed, humans conveyed their emotions through facial expressions. This phenomenon is universally recognized across cultures; emotions like joy, sadness, anger, and surprise are instinctively expressed. For instance, a smile universally signifies happiness and goodwill, while a frown denotes dissatisfaction or distress. These nonverbal signals significantly enhance emotional connections and foster mutual understanding. In forensic science, facial expressions are analyzed as potential indicators of deception, suggesting that they reveal instinctive feelings that are hard for individuals to conceal. Thus, facial expressions are a vital component of human interaction and represent the most primitive form of communication that transcends linguistic limitations.

In Korea, the significance of facial expressions is particularly pronounced. As a "high-context society," Korea relies heavily on implicit messages and nonverbal cues. Effective communication in this context requires not just understanding spoken words but also grasping the subtle nuances conveyed through tone and facial expressions. Essentially, it is crucial to read the mood beyond the verbal message. Moreover, the collectivist nature of Korean culture emphasizes the importance of relationships; understanding others' emotions through facial expressions is fundamental to maintaining harmonious connections.

The term "facial expression illiterate" describes an individual who struggles to read or interpret others' facial expressions. The need for effective, friendly communication has become increasingly evident in the wake of the COVID-19 pandemic, during which masks hindered face-to-face interaction. This lack of visual cues made it challenging for people to empathize with one another, leading to increased social isolation and a renewed appreciation for nonverbal communication. In the context of video conferences and calls, facial expressions have played a crucial role in conveying emotions and fostering social bonds. Our experiences during the pandemic have reinforced the understanding that nonverbal communication is vital for providing social connections and psychological support, serving as the foundation of human relationships.

The growing interest in human faces by technology stems from a desire to engage with users in a more human manner. In the era of generative AI, technological advancements increasingly aim to replicate human characteristics, emphasizing the importance of understanding and responding to human emotions through facial expressions.

The Power of Affordance in the Age of Explosive New Technology

Facial expressions have long been significant since the early evolution of Homo sapiens. However, in today's era of rapidly advancing technology, their importance has magnified due to the concept of "affordance," which facilitates user interaction with artificial objects.

Understanding affordance

In modern technological society, humans frequently interact with devices such as computers and robots. For effective usage, it's crucial that users can easily request certain actions and comprehend how to utilize these technologies without extensive training. This interaction relies heavily on considerations of user interface (UI). At the core of any effective UI are its "affordances," which refer to the design elements that allow users to recognize and use a product intuitively.

The term "affordance" was first introduced in 1977 by American psychologist James J. Gibson, who defined it as a phenomenon where objects provide cues that suggest how they can be used. For instance, if you encounter a coffee maker in a foreign hotel and struggle to operate it, this indicates poor affordance. Conversely, visual guidance cues, like the pink or green lines painted at road intersections, enhance usability and demonstrate good affordance.

Types of affordances

Affordances can be categorized into three main types:

1. *Cognitive affordances*: These are elements that increase perceptibility. For example, pink and green guidance lines on roads help drivers navigate safely by indicating correct lane usage. Such features improve recognition during high-speed driving and enhance overall safety. Another common example is parking lot vacancy lights: red signals that a space is occupied, while green indicates availability. This visual cue allows drivers to quickly assess parking options from a distance, reducing the time spent searching for a spot.

2. *Physical affordances*: These enhance the possibility for action. For example, CPTED (Crime Prevention Through Environmental Design) principles advocate for the strategic placement of windows in dark alleys to increase visibility and deter crime. Similarly, snack packaging often includes grooves designed for easy tearing and access, demonstrating thoughtful physical affordance.

3. *Virtual affordances*: These simplify the context of use. A

prime example is the process of transferring money via mobile banking. Traditional methods often require users to select their bank before entering the account number. However, platforms like Toss have improved usability by allowing users to input the account number first, thereby enhancing the overall user experience (UX).

Affordances have become increasingly crucial in today's rapidly evolving technological landscape. With a constant influx of new technologies, products, and services, users often encounter unfamiliar interfaces. Regardless of a product's quality or sophistication, it becomes ineffective if consumers cannot intuitively navigate and use it.

So, what is the most fundamental and straightforward form of affordance? The answer lies in the face and its expressions. As the world embraces advanced technologies, face tech emerges as a pivotal element in enhancing UI. By utilizing facial recognition and expression analysis, technology can create more intuitive and relatable experiences, bridging the gap between human emotions and machine interfaces. This shift towards incorporating human-like interactions is essential for ensuring that new technologies resonate with users and facilitate seamless engagement.

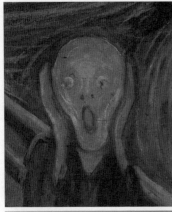
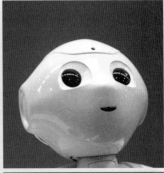

- Technology gains a face.
- Technology expresses emotions.
- The best communication tool is
  the face itself.

Humanize Technology with Face Tech

How will technology make its "first impression"?
Will it communicate through facial expressions, offer simple information, or engage via voice or touch?
The size of a touchscreen also matters – how can it be designed to reduce psychological burden and enhance user convenience?

Many companies are exploring human facial expressions to answer these questions. In the future, the ability to read and respond to human emotions will become a key differentiator for businesses and products. Face tech emerges as a powerful tool that can provide a competitive edge in a landscape teeming with new technologies. From creating and analyzing facial expressions to crafting unique UX, face tech offers a pathway for innovation.

Face tech can simplify learning for users through intuitive design, decreasing the need for extensive user support and training. When users can troubleshoot on their own, companies can save costs and improve efficiency. Additionally, intuitive technology helps products stand out in a saturated market. In an era where users have numerous alternatives, a user-friendly interface can become a significant brand differentiator.

With the increasing fatigue from technology overload, effective communication between technology and users is more vital than the technology itself. To build an inclusive AI society, we must consider affordances to ensure that technology is accessible to everyone, including those who may struggle with digital tools. This involves continuous effort to enhance digital affordances, making AI technologies more applicable in real-world scenarios.

The application of face tech also reflects cultural differences. According to Trompenaars' model of national cultural differences, there is an intriguing relationship between the use of emoticons and the emotional expressiveness of cultures. In cultures like Japan and China, where emotional expression is often restrained, individuals tend to use emoticons more actively. This phenomenon can be attributed to the challenge of conveying emotions clearly in environments where direct emotional expression is less common. In these societies, people often find it difficult to articulate their feelings openly, leading to an increased reliance on mobile emoticons. Emoticons serve as a valuable tool for indirectly expressing emotional states, providing a means to communicate complex feelings and nuanced situations without the need for explicit verbalization. The widespread use of emoticons in Asia reflects a cultural adaptation that allows individuals to navigate the intricacies of emotional communication more effectively.

This phenomenon also resonates with generational shifts. Generation Zalpha (Gen Z + Gen Alpha) is characterized by a preference for digital communication over traditional face-to-face interactions. As this generation becomes more prominent, their comfort with technology and visual communication will likely enhance their engagement with face tech.

Members of Generation Zalpa prioritize images over text, videos over images, and atmosphere over mere facts. They gravitate toward platforms and technologies that allow for friendly, visually rich interactions. Face tech aligns perfectly with their communication preferences, enabling them to express themselves and connect with others in innovative ways.

In the 1970s, Japanese roboticist Masahiro Mori introduced the concept of the "uncanny valley," which describes how robots or AI creations that closely resemble humans can evoke feelings of eeriness or discomfort when they fail to perfectly mimic human characteristics. This phenomenon arises from the strange familiarity and discomfort that imperfectly human-like objects elicit, leading to a negative emotional response. Fast forward to 2025, and significant advancements in face tech have started to bridge this uncanny divide. Modern technology enables the creation of robots and AI systems that exhibit well-refined and realistic facial expressions, making them appear more natural and relatable. This evolution addresses the uncanny valley by enhancing the realism of humanoid robots, allowing them to engage more effectively with humans.

The materialization and humanization of technology are emerging as fundamental paradigms in a world increasingly influenced by generative AI. As technology becomes more integrated into our daily lives, conveying human-like emotions through facial expressions becomes essential. This humanization not only improves user interaction but also fosters emotional connections between humans and machines.

There's a saying: "A good countenance is a letter of recommendation." This adage highlights the importance of sincerity conveyed through facial expressions – not just in people but in products as well. As we consider our approach to technology and user interaction, we must reflect on the expressions our products convey to customers. What face are you showing to the world?

Embracing
Harmlessness

People today love things that are small, cute, a little bit clumsy, but pure. What these traits have in common is that they are harmless – they don't cause stress or provoke criticism, and they don't make anyone feel the need to oppose them. We call this characteristic "harmlessness," and we believe it explains why such things have become increasingly appealing. Beloved animals like baby panda Fu Bao, the trend of making everything miniature, and the popularity of awkward speech and roughly drawn emoticons all stem from this idea of harmlessness.

Harmlessness isn't just about being pretty. Young people, weary from economic hardships, an uncertain future, deepening social and political conflicts, and the emotional toll of the pandemic, often describe themselves as the "scratched generation." In response to this gloom, they seek out cute, pure, and simple things that cause no harm.

We shouldn't view harmlessness as merely the absence of negativity. It's important to understand the historical context and characteristics that make harmless things so valued. In today's chaotic world, harmlessness has become a key to survival.

The athlete who captured the most attention at the 2024 Paris Olympics was Kim Ye-ji, the silver medalist in the 10m air pistol shooting event. Her futuristic equipment, all-black outfit, and cool, unwavering expression earned her the title of "the Paris Olympics' coolest athlete" from *The New York Times*. Even Tesla founder Elon Musk commented, "She could be cast in an action movie. No acting required!" But the buzz didn't stop there. Despite her "cold-blooded killer" image reminiscent of a noir film, she appeared at the event with a towel adorned with a cute elephant doll – a gift from her 5-year-old daughter. This unexpected charm made her a hot topic throughout the Olympics. A cold-blooded killer with a cute elephant doll!

Kim Ye-ji's story is part of a broader trend. Many young people today attach keychains or small dolls to their backpacks, with some even hanging inexpensive dolls on luxury bags worth thousands of dollars. As love for dolls grows among students, their photos have shifted from "life shots인생샷" to "doll shots인형샷." In response, fancy stationery store chain Artbox released special doll clothes, glasses, bracelets, and other accessories, which became extremely popular.

The case of Sylvanian characters is particularly interesting. Sylvanian is a series of miniature figures created by the Japanese toy company EPOCH in 1985, depicting the lives of middle-class animal families living in the English countryside. The collection includes not just dolls like rabbits, cats, and squirrels, but also furniture and appliances to complete their homes. Sylvanian, which has been available in the Korean market since 2008, began selling through Artbox's online and offline channels in 2021. Initially, it didn't gain much attention, but since its resale in 2024, it has surged in popularity, leading to "open runs" and being completely sold out. According to Shinhan Card's Big Data Research Institute, the number of doll key ring prop shops in 2024 increased by about 112% compared to 2022, with forty to fifty-somethings making up 28% of prop shop customers. This highlights the widespread appeal of cute items across all ages.

It's not just key rings: pop-up stores, goods, and trending items today are overwhelmingly cute and adorable. The panda bear Fu Bao, often lovingly called a "cute genius," has captivated the entire nation with her every move. While everyone appreciates cute things, the current craze for such items is extraordinary. These small, cute, and innocent things can be characterized as harmless. The phenomenon where the appeal of these harmless items becomes increasingly influential is termed "harmlessness무해력."

The common trait of harmless beings and things is that they don't cause stress or provoke opposition; they don't give me a reason to criticize them. But why are harmless things so popular? It's likely because life has become increasingly difficult. With the ongoing recession and the harsh reality that offers little hope for a better tomorrow, people are seeking comfort. Meanwhile, political and social conflicts – over ideology, class, generations, and gender – are deepening, and competition is intensifying. Amid these challenges, harmless things create a psychological safety zone. Whether people are drawn to them because they're cute or because the world feels chaotic, harmless things have become incredibly popular.

Various Forms of Harmlessness

1. Small and harmless

Once upon a time, a child was more fascinated by the tiny carp-shaped soy sauce container that came with sashimi than by the sashimi itself. That child grew up and began creating dolls of the soy sauce container and its friends.

This is the story behind Mimools미물즈 (@mimools.kr), a brand that has become a sensation on Instagram for its adorable small objects. The word "*mimool*" means "tiny thing" or "creature" in Korean, and the brand evokes nostalgia, reminding many of the small umbrellas or carp-shaped soy sauce containers they might have saved from sushi boxes. There's something inherently charming about small things – even ordinary objects become cute and endearing when miniaturized. Their smallness gives a sense of safety, which is why tiny items are so popular these days.

Mimools offers "handmade creations inspired by small beings," such as old-fashioned candy, honey rice cakes, and fish. These tiny dolls have become a perfect comfort item for adults. By turning the small soy sauce container into a doll and giving it pickled vegetables and wasabi as companions, Mimools is gradually building a universe of tiny things.

While abundance is usually prized, some items are more popular precisely because they are small. For example, "micro cakes," which are less than 5 centimeters in diameter, are gaining attention. Also called "bite cakes한입 케이크," they're small enough to fit in the palm of your hand but still feature all the elements of a full-sized cake, with dense decorations that add to their cuteness. In April 2024, Starbucks introduced a bite-sized finger food called "Petit Canelé," further proving that small, "harmless" foods are winning over consumers.

As the love for small things grows, the miniature market is thriving. Once considered niche collectibles, miniatures are now embraced as part of Gen Z's "kidult" culture. In July 2024, the toy maker Sonokong손오공 launched "Minibus," a miniature brand from the global toy company MGA. The first products released include the "Home Appliance Series," where you can create your own home café with tiny espresso machines, milk tea makers, juicers, and soda machines, as well as the "Lifestyle Series," featuring mini fish tanks, flowerpots, and candles.

Gachapon shops, which sell small capsule toys, are also enjoying great popularity. The term "*gacha*" comes from the Japanese word "*gacha gacha*ガチャガチャ," mimicking the clinking sound of metal as you insert a coin into a capsule toy machine and turn the lever to receive the capsule (*pon*). These small capsules, which fit in the palm of your hand, contain a variety of toys like mini figures, dolls, and stationery. The *gachapon* store that opened in Jamsil in February 2024 was a huge hit, selling mini key rings of popular characters from Sanrio, Crayon Shin-chan, and Chiikawa, along with soft, squishy toys. Due to the ongoing kidult craze, a new branch opened in Hongdae in April 2024, where *gachapon* machines featuring popular characters sold out immediately.

After the beloved Everland panda Fu Bao left the country, the spotlight turned to the red panda. By March 2024, the official channel for Everland's red panda, "Ogugreseo오구그레서," had garnered over 4 million cumulative views. The red panda, much smaller than a regular panda, is known for its non-threatening behavior – its most aggressive act is standing on its hind legs and appearing to say "Hurrah!만세!" As an internationally endangered species (Appendix 1 in CITES) with fewer than 10,000 left in the world, its rarity only deepens the affection people feel for this charming animal.

Small pets are becoming increasingly popular. While Korea has traditionally favored small dog breeds like Malteses and Poodles, there is now growing interest in even tinier pets, such as hamsters. With this rise in popularity, content related to small animals has also seen a surge. A prime example is SBSTV Animal Farm's official YouTube channel series "Zocomi Animal Hospital" (Zocomi쪼꼬미 means "tiny and small" in Korean), which recently launched its fourth season. The series features a veterinarian treating and caring for small, rare animals in Korea, such as prairie dogs, degus, sugar gliders, guinea pigs, meerkats, and Balkan terrapins. Episodes 1 to 12 have become especially popular, amassing 3.8 million views and sparking widespread interest.

2. Cute and harmless

The second category of harmlessness includes pretty and cute items. For instance, keyboard enthusiasts often customize their keyboards by lubricating them or adding reinforcement plates to achieve the perfect key feel and sound. Recently, however, there has been a growing trend of customizing keyboards with keycaps shaped like small dolls or cute characters – not just for functionality, but to create an aesthetically pleasing keyboard. This trend highlights how the interest in pretty things is extending even to keyboards, which are typically valued for their practicality alone.

The cheese shop "Your Naked Cheese" (@yournakedcheese), with locations in Seongsu-dong, Seoul, and Haeundae, Busan, is well-known for its beautiful and cute cheese and wine presentations. The summer cheese platter, which pays homage to the season with gouda, brunost, Colby-Jack, and pepper jack, is so visually appealing that it's almost a shame to eat it.

In Mapo-gu, Seoul, the "Fresh Plush" store offers dog toys in a grocery market setting. From a distance, the store presents a stunning visual reminiscent of an American mart. The adorable designs, featuring snacks, milk, and sauces, not only delight dogs but also capture the hearts of their owners. Additionally, it serves as a studio where you can photograph your dog in a shopping basket, creating a delightful blend of small pets and cute toys. This combination represents a harmless way to enjoy both pets and playful designs.

3. Harmless because it's awkward

The awkwardly spoken Korean of Hani (real name Pam Hani), a member of the popular girl group New Jeans, has become a hot topic among netizens. Fans affectionately refer to her unique way of speaking as "*Pamguk-eo*팜국어," a playful twist on "*Han-guk-eo*한국어," meaning "Korean," as well as "Pamturi팜투리," a parody of "*saturi*사투리," meaning "local dialect." Hani's innocent and pure awkwardness is seen as harmless.

As an all-around entertainer with impressive skills in danc-ing, singing, and English, Hani is Vietnamese-Australian and re-portedly faced challenges learning Korean when she first debuted with the group. However, both her fellow New Jeans members and fans appreciate her dedication to mastering the language.

Much like a mother who understands her child's babbling, they easily forgive her small mistakes, embracing them as endearing quirks. This reflects the idea that unintentional mistakes are harmless. The awkwardness that is both pure and lovable can be described as "pure and carefree harmlessness."

Harmlessness can sometimes stem from a lack of experience. A great example is the Instagram page "Grandma's Happy Life슬기로운 할매생활" (@halmae_love), where grandmothers and grandfathers cook foreign dishes. "*Monggeul monggeul*" translates to "a lumpy and squashy state," perfectly capturing the channel's charm. The main content features elderly amateur chefs trying their hand at dishes they've never encountered before, such as Middle Eastern hummus, Italian gnocchi and lasagna, and Chinese menbosha. Their playful attempts to recite the lasagna recipe in a Jeju dialect and their innocent curiosity about unfamiliar menu items evoke a childlike innocence.

Similarly, actor Kim Suk-hoon, selected as an Eco-Friend of the 2024 Seoul International Environmental Film Festival, embodies harmlessness through his persona as "Mr. Ssujeossi쓰저씨" (a blend of 쓰레기, meaning "trash," and 아저씨, meaning "uncle"). He receives positive feedback for sharing his daily routine of picking up trash on his YouTube channel, "My Trash Uncle나의 쓰레기 아저씨." Many admire his dedication to helping the environment and express in the comments their willingness to join his efforts, reinforcing the idea that even gentle, innocent actions can be perceived as harmless yet impactful.

Is there anything purer than nature? The Seoul Botanic Park, which was newly renovated in May 2019, has attracted 20 million visitors in just four years since opening, with numbers projected to double in 2024 compared to the previous year. This expansive urban botanical garden, covering the area of 70 soccer fields, has become a hotspot for plant lovers, showcasing not only native Korean plants but also species from 12 cities around the world.

Videos featuring nature are also gaining popularity. For instance, the Jeju Contents Agency제주영상·문화산업진흥원 has been providing free 4K high-resolution videos of Jeju Island's stunning scenery since 2022. These videos have been featured in numerous TV programs and films and are widely appreciated by the public. On platforms like YouTube, high-quality 12K nature videos often attract viewers who watch them for 3-4 hours at a time.

Interestingly, items that appear simple or roughly made yet maintain a friendly quality are also considered harmless. A prime example is the remarkable popularity in Korea of the Japanese illustrator "KAWAISONI!" and their character, "Panchu Rabbit" (@opanchu.usagi). They released a collaboration edition with skincare company Mediheal and even hosted pop-up stores in popular locations like The Hyundai Seoul and Myeongdong. However, upon closer inspection, the character's design is somewhat lacking in refinement. Many trending characters and popular emoticons share this rough aesthetic, resembling quick

- Small, cute, and harmless.
- Pretty, lovable, and harmless.
- The immense power that comes from being extremely fragile.

doodles rather than polished artwork.

Even in the KakaoTalk emoticon shop, roughly drawn designs are favored. The keyword search results reveal that terms like "roughly대충" have 126 entries, and "insignificant하찮은" has 208 entries, surpassing common search phrases like "hello" and "what are you doing." The so-called "insignificant series" emoticons, such as "broken bear망그러진곰," are becoming increasingly popular. These "insignificant" emoticons resonate with users due to their familiar charm, reminiscent of casual doodles in a notepad. They possess an appeal that is both rough around the edges and comfortably beyond conventional standards, making them endearing in their simplicity.

How Does Harmlessness Have Power?

The concept of harmlessness presents a paradox. While it suggests the absence of harm and implies minimal influence on others, it also embodies a certain power that can affect those around it. How can something deemed harmless possess such power?

Harmlessness can be broken down into four elements: smallness, cuteness, innocence, and clumsiness. The ultimate embodiment of all these elements of harmlessness is a baby. Babies are small, cute, innocent, and often clumsy, disarming us completely when we encounter them.

From an evolutionary psychology perspective, it is suggested that the more parental care a species requires, the cuter its off-spring tend to be. This evolutionary trait ensures that adults are more likely to provide care to those who appear cute. British psychologist Kevin Dutton states that when we see a baby's image, the part of our brain that controls pleasure is instantly activated, highlighting that children are the most powerful persuaders for care.

Research by Gary Genosko reveals common characteristics that trigger our protective instincts toward babies, such as (1) a head size of a certain proportion to the body, (2) a wide forehead with large eyes, and (3) round, chubby limbs and body shape. These traits are collectively referred to as the "baby schema," which Disney characters like Mickey Mouse and Bambi often exaggerate to enhance their appeal.

Ethologist Konrad Lorenz further explains that when baby-like features are present in fictional characters, we experience similar emotions to those elicited by real babies. This is why beloved characters and small pets often evoke feelings akin to those we have for human infants. In essence, harmless beings like babies awaken our instinct to nurture and care for them.

Caring for someone implies a position of superiority over that entity. Specifically, small objects that embody this kind of harmlessness naturally feel benign because they are smaller than I am and therefore less likely to pose a threat. The same applies to the variety of harmlessness brought about by cute things. Professor Kwon Yuria권유리아 suggests that cuteness reflects "the feeling of power that the strong experience toward the weak." In other words, when we gaze upon small and cute objects like miniatures, "we observe them with a superior perspective while feeling joy, and this affection stems from the assurance that they are non-threatening." The foundation of our affectionate feelings for small and cute things is rooted in the relief felt when we know they are harmless.

Pure and simple harmlessness can also be understood similarly. John Sweller's "cognitive load theory" posits that human cognitive resources are limited, meaning simple things are easier to comprehend and process than complex ones. In today's information age, individuals exposed to a vast array of stimulating information often suffer from digital fatigue and mental strain. Their efforts to heal through pure and innocent objects, even if imperfect, can be interpreted as a preference for simple and unrefined items. In essence, owning or cherishing harmless objects is the easiest way for us to reaffirm our sense of relief and control in our daily lives. This sense of control becomes increasingly vital in modern society, where family bonds and social connections are weakening. Consequently, young people, who may feel relatively powerless in social dynamics, often gravitate toward cute items. Additionally, it is known that cute beings release oxytocin, promoting a feeling of connection and reducing cortisol, the stress hormone. When my environment is challenging and stress levels rise, I instinctively seek out harmless beings that are small, cute, pure, and thus clearly vulnerable and unlikely to harm me, as a means of relief.

Outlook and Implications

The passions of a society's members often reveal the elements that the community lacks the most. The current prevalence of harmlessness in Korean society may indicate the extent to which our community is experiencing pain. In fact, the younger generation now refers to themselves as the "scratched generation긁힌 세대." They frequently use the term "scratched" to describe instances when they've been picked on and their pride wounded. When they feel scratched, they experience genuine hurt. Perhaps we are in an era where we desperately need something harmless to heal these scratched wounds or something that alleviates the irritations of life without causing any further injury.

What causes these scratches? There are numerous factors. As mentioned briefly in the introduction, the economy is struggling. With high prices and elevated interest rates, consumer spending has decreased, leading to sluggish domestic demand, and self-employed individuals face particularly severe challenges. This may not be merely a temporary economic downturn. As low growth becomes entrenched, it is increasingly difficult to maintain an optimistic outlook that tomorrow will be better than today. This represents a significant turning point that distinguishes the values of the older generations, who experienced youth

during a time of robust growth, from those of the younger generations. There exists a substantial gap in the perception that no
matter how hard one strives, social mobility is nearly impossible
without advantages such as good looks or a wealthy background.

Depression is evolving into anger. At the core of this anger
lies the escalating conflict within the country. As the divide between generations and socioeconomic classes deepens, chronic
ideological disputes are intensifying daily, and recently, the ani-
mosity between men and women has reached an alarming level
that cannot be overlooked.

Additionally, it is important to highlight the rise of digital
fatigue. The myriad new technologies emerging daily are forcing
us to disconnect from our familiar lives. With an overwhelming
amount of information flooding various platforms and devices,
doubts about our choices are increasingly prevalent. The content
we encounter each day is significantly stimulating. In this context, it is only natural to seek out harmless, low-stimulation items
and content that can alleviate this digital exhaustion.

In conclusion, the trend toward harmlessness can be interpreted as a yearning for something that heals our hearts and clar-
ifies our thoughts in an era rife with conflict, where stimulation
is ubiquitous, and sharp blades are pointed at one another. Even
if this harmless trend reflects underlying socio-economic issues,
it remains valuable to explore the meaning this tendency presents
us. What should we focus on moving forward?

The first challenge is how authentically we can communicate

our organization's harmless image in an era of conflict. Recently, digital humans, adorable children, and charming animals have been frequently featured as advertising models. These "harmless models" avoid social controversies such as drunk driving or drug use. Today's consumers are ruthless: when issues arise, they unleash a torrent of malicious comments and can swiftly condemn a brand.

In this environment, the preference for harmless models is likely to intensify as a means to protect brand image. However, this extends beyond just advertising models. Creating a harmless image for a company or organization poses an even greater challenge. As the emphasis on social responsibility, including ESG initiatives, has increased, many organizations are voicing their positions on social issues and highlighting their efforts to address them. Yet, achieving meaningful change in a short time frame is not easy, leading to temptations for quick fixes.

Examples include "greenwashing," which pretends to prioritize environmental protection while obscuring or minimizing negative impacts; "AI-washing," which claims to employ AI technology while relying on basic algorithms; and "pink-washing," which involves misleading marketing that falsely supports the LGBTQ+ community. When the truth behind these "washings" is exposed, consumer backlash is fierce. Sincerity is crucial in these promotional efforts. If genuine intentions cannot be established, silence may be the better option. Harmlessness is attainable only through pure intentions.

Second, it must be emphasized that harmlessness is not synonymous with "lack of charm." Harmless entities should not be viewed merely as the "absence of negativity." This absence can imply that they are unremarkable objects lacking appeal or competitiveness and fail to provide any stimulation. We need to accurately understand the historical context and characteristics that have led to the rise of harmless entities and devise effective strategies that leverage harmlessness.

Additionally, we should recognize that artificial cuteness – such as childish regression or awkward *aegyo* – does not guarantee popularity. Just as achieving simple design is a formidable challenge, creating cuteness that embodies childlike innocence is equally complex. Only authentic cuteness, backed by a clear grasp of trends and a deep understanding of consumer preferences, can genuinely engage consumers. This is a crucial consideration when developing various products or characters.

The label "harmless" predominantly applied to food that is safe for the human body, but its usage has expanded significantly in recent times. The "do no harm" principle was applied as a safety standard in the development of COVID-19 vaccines and has become a fundamental ethical guideline across various fields, including artificial intelligence, automated driving, life sciences, and environmental protection. Moreover, it has become a term widely used for content and people, with phrases like "harmless entertainment," "harmless drama," "harmless combinations," and "harmless number two" becoming commonplace. If you search for the term "harmless" in an online bookstore, you'll find numerous titles such as *Harmless People*, *Harmless Human Relationships*, *Harmless Islam*, and *Harmless Money Making* appearing one after another. We are in a golden age of harmlessness. As mentioned earlier, the emphasis on harmlessness suggests a prevalence of things that threaten us. Harmlessness is not merely about cute design; it has become essential for survival in this overwhelming world.

Shifting
Gradation of
Korean Culture

As various Korean products and exports like K-pop, K-food, and K-dramas gain international prominence, the number of foreign residents in Korea has reached a milestone, exceeding 2.5 million and nearing 5% of the population. In this context, answering the question, "What is truly Korean?" becomes more complex. For a long time, Korea has held the belief, or sense of pride, that it is one of the few nations where a single ethnic group makes up the entire population. However, in an era of large-scale migration and global social media, where tastes and trends are shared across borders, defining the "K" component based on a single standard is becoming increasingly difficult. To address this, the concept of "gradation K" has been introduced, suggesting that Korean identity should be viewed through the lens of gradation, or a gradient, where one color transitions into another. The line between Korean and global culture is becoming increasingly blurred, not just in content and food but also in urban environments. For businesses, new markets have emerged, targeting foreign residents, tourists, and overseas consumers. Gradation K offers various industrial and cultural insights. It is time for a more flexible conversation about "what is truly Korean."

The six members of the new girl group VCHA, named by the Grammy's news division as one of the "25 Artists to Watch in 2024," are all fluent in English. Lexi, Cage, Savannah, and Kendall are American, Camila is Canadian, and Kaylee holds dual citizenship in Korea and the United States. The production team is equally international, featuring Lauren Aquilina, who has written hits for global stars like Little Mix and Demi Lovato, along with Marcus Andersson and Chloe Latimer. VCHA is a project by JYP Entertainment, spearheaded by founder Park Jin-young. But can VCHA truly be called "K-pop"? How far does K-pop extend? Can it only retain the "K" when all members are Korean, the album is produced domestically and is then exported internationally? How about "K-pop 2.0," where international members are recruited, and local companies handle promotions and performances?

Going one step further, what if all members are from different countries and the entire process of discovery, training, production and debuting artists is done with local partners through the Korean system. Is this, let's say, "K-pop 3.0," still considered K-pop? Even before VCHA, JYP Entertainment had already introduced

NiziU and Boy Story, groups made up entirely of local members from Japan and China, respectively, and has recently established "JYP Latin America" to develop a girl group hailing from that continent. So, let's revisit the question: How "K" is VCHA?

When something cannot be strictly classified as black or white, but exists in the spectrum between them, we use the term "gradation." As a physical term meaning "a property observed during an object's transition from one stage to another," it's now commonly used in areas like nail art, dyeing, and makeup. Rather than signifying a distinct color, it represents the gradual shift from one color to another. Nature itself is a gradation. Consider the sunset painting the sky – can we label that mysteriously spreading color as simply red or blue? If JYP's Wonder Girls, whose earnest entry into the U.S. market in 2009 can be symbolized with a bold "K," could VCHA, with its thorough localization, represent a softer "K"? In this sense, "K" is not binary but continuous – a gradation.

The question of "What is K, or Korean?" should now be approached through a gradation concept rather than answered with a simple "this is" or "that isn't." Based on this understanding, *2025 K-Consumer Trend Insights* proposes the term "gradation K" to describe this evolving aspect of Korean identity. The gradation K trend reflects Korea's ongoing expansion of its national identity as it transitions into a multiethnic, multicultural society, while deeply engaging with the world and exchanging economic and cultural influences. In the past, there was the stereotype and sense of pride felt by Koreans when viewing their country as one of the few nations with a single ethnic group. Today, however, Korea is recognized as a multicultural nation. The OECD defines countries with foreign populations exceeding 5% as multicultural, and Korea's foreign residents now surpass 2.5 million, accounting for 5% of the population. Beyond K-pop, Korean culture – encompassing food, mobile and video games, convenience stores, urban systems, and various other forms of content – continues to take root globally. Markets catering to foreigners are also growing, with increasing economic impact. These shifts can be explored through three aspects of gradation: people gradation, culture gradation, and market gradation.

People Gradation

"Who is Korean?"

Imagine being asked this question alongside four job cards showing an Indian painter, an Asian chef, a Latino doctor, and a European farmer. How would you answer? The correct response is, "I don't know." This question is actually used as a teaching tool in multicultural education for elementary students. The approach to multicultural education has evolved, moving beyond simply acknowledging differences in appearance, to teaching that nationality should not be determined by looks at all. We are entering an era where being Korean cannot be defined by race alone – a phenomenon that can be termed "people gradation," reflecting the shifting concept of the Korean people.

In Eumseong, North Chungcheong Province, 16% of the population is foreign – one in six people. The economy of Eumseong, which is grappling with aging, would struggle to function without its foreign population. In some restaurants, you might say "Namaste" upon entering and hear "Namaste" in return. Eumseong is not unique; this is a broader social shift Korea is facing as it deals with low birth rates, aging, and population decline.

Schools, where all children gather, offer a glimpse into this emerging era of people gradation. At an elementary school in Ansan, Gyeonggi Province, 97.4% of students are from immigrant backgrounds; that is, out of 100 students only three are "Korean" in the traditional, ethnic sense. Across the country, there are 350 schools where over 30% of the students are from multicultural families. As the number of multicultural students rises, especially with Korea's declining birth rate, this percentage will likely grow.

Schools in this multicultural era are adapting their educational methods. Now, students are classified not by nationality or race, but by their proficiency in Korean. Special attention is given to ensuring language doesn't hinder a student's education. For those in multicultural classes, evaluations are adjusted based on their Korean language skills, ensuring they have equal educational opportunities. Tests are often provided in languages the students are more familiar with, minimizing the impact of language barriers on academic performance. Additionally, some schools send newsletters home in languages like Mongolian, Russian, and Chinese to assist parents who are not fluent in Korean. In Jeollanam Province, the Office of Education even offers a multilingual translation service to translate notices and educational materials for parents into various languages.

Multicultural education is also provided to Korean students. Multicultural special classes serve as spaces where students from immigrant families can learn about Korean culture while also providing Korean students an opportunity to understand other countries. In one class in Bucheon, traditional costumes from various nations are displayed on the walls and are used during the school's "Intercultural Understanding Week." During this time, multicultural students introduce their heritage to their Korean classmates, fostering mutual understanding. Some schools even hold multilingual camps where students learn the languages spoken by their peers. This approach shifts education from merely understanding "the other" to promoting mutual cultural exchange.

Multicultural integration extends beyond schools into the workplace. It is increasingly common to work alongside foreign colleagues, not just in simple labor roles, but in key positions aimed at elevating Korean companies on the global stage. For instance, Samyang Foods, known worldwide for its Buldak

Bokkeum Ramen불닭볶음면, has launched major global talent recruitment efforts, with overseas sales making up 78% of its total revenue. Similarly, Hyundai Motor Company has benefitted from its foreign division, which includes around 70 international executives and employees, like the global Chief Operating Officer (COO), Chief Design Officer (CDO), and Chief Creative Officer (CCO), who are spearheading its global expansion.

Domestic startups targeting global markets are also actively seeking foreign talent. At Seoul Robotics, an autonomous driving software company, 23 of its 55 employees are foreigners, and the head of HR is German. This international diversity helps the company communicate effectively with its key clients, many of which are German companies. Such changes are becoming a trend in recruitment. Skills and job fit are now more important than nationality. When Korean companies expand abroad, the language skills and cultural knowledge of foreign employees become assets for success.

In a survey conducted by Job Korea and KLiK, a foreign recruitment service, 61.5% of respondents predicted an increase in hiring foreign talent. Most workers who have already worked with foreign colleagues are embracing this change. Only 10% expressed resistance to working with foreign colleagues, while many see the benefit of learning about different cultures and gaining new perspectives on work.

To ensure a comfortable living standard for foreign employees, who have been recruited with great effort, companies are increasing their support and consideration. One of the primary areas of focus is providing global menu options for employees who are either not keen on Korean food or cannot eat certain ingredients for religious reasons. For instance, Samsung Electronics' cafeteria always offers an Indian corner alongside Korean, Chinese, and Japanese dishes, with 100% halal-certified meat sourced from the start. HD Hyundai Heavy Industries provides alcohol- and pork-free meals for its Muslim employees, along with separate take-home meal packages for iftar during Ramadan.

Language support is also becoming essential for smooth communication, especially in environments where communication impacts safety. In the construction industry, for example, companies are addressing safety issues by providing multilingual instructions like "Connect the safety belt" in languages such as Chinese, Vietnamese, and Burmese. Hyundai Engineering & Construction has developed a multilingual translation app called "Mobile HPMS," which instantly translates everyday and work-related conversations into five languages, improving communication at construction sites. Similarly, Coupang employs around 250 full-time interpreters and translators to facilitate both internal communication and remote meetings with overseas offices. Some companies even partner with interpretation and translation graduate schools to secure specialized staff.

Since not all companies can manage communication challenges alone, startups have emerged to fill this gap. Kstart (kstart.

co.kr), for example, provides life-oriented services, including ac- companying foreigners to government offices or banks to assist with daily life challenges. Literacy M, a health management app, offers medical services to foreign residents by providing person- al health records in their native language.

Migrant communities also play a vital role in the lives of international residents in Korea. A notable example is the Philippine market, which opens every Sunday at 1 p.m. near Hy- ehwa-dong Cathedral. Similarly, Ansan City hosts the Songkran Festival, Cambodia's biggest holiday, catering to the Cambodian community in Korea.

While the number of immigrants entering Korea has risen, many Koreans are also venturing abroad. Korea ranks third, after China and India, in the number of international students studying in the U.S., highlighting how many Koreans are seeking opportu- nities overseas despite the larger populations of China and India.

Cultural Gradation

"Have you heard of Mongtan New Town?"

Imagine a Korean-style apartment complex with 1,000 house- holds, Korean convenience stores like CU and GS25 on every corner, café chains such as Tom N Toms and Caffe Bene, street vendors selling *tteokbokki* and fish cakes, and even signs in Korean. This scene is not from Korea but Ulaanbaatar, the capital of Mongolia. The area, resembling Gyeonggi Province's Dongtan New Town, has been nicknamed "Mongtan" by Korean tourists. It's not just the city's appearance that mirrors Korea; inside convenience stores, Mongolians can be seen enjoying kimbap and cup ramen, while cafés bustle with people working on laptops, just like in Korean cafés. Korean culture has deeply woven itself into Mongolian daily life, extending beyond the mere export of products to what some call a "transplanting" of culture.

This blending of cultures, where Korean traditions become global and vice versa, reflects the second type of gradation K: "cultural gradation." Korean-style urban systems are also spreading internationally. For example, the governments of Korea and Vietnam signed an MOU on urban-housing development to help develop Bac Ninh Province, aiming to create a "Pangyo New City"-style urban space and build 1 million social housing units. Vietnam already has a strong system of "K-distribution," with Korean companies leading in sectors such as shopping malls, movie theaters, fast food, and convenience stores. If the urban development plan moves forward, it could establish a model for exporting the Korean-style urban system abroad, beyond just housing construction.

Even Korean security capabilities are being exported. In September 2024, Guatemala opened a "Police Job Training Center" to learn from Korean expertise. The transfer of skills includes cyber investigation, forensic science investigation techniques,

미래의창

도서목록

홈페이지 **miraebook.co.kr**
페이스북 **facebook.com/miraebook**
인스타그램 **@miraebook**

미래의창

바이킹에서 메이플라워 호까지,
콜럼버스에서 일론 머스크까지
세계사의 주역은 언제나 이주민들이었다!

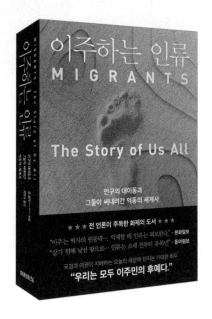

이주하는 인류
인구의 대이동과 그들이 써내려간 역동의 세계사

샘 밀러 지음 | 최정숙 옮김 | 424쪽 | 19,000원

인류의 뿌리, 이주의 역사를 탐험하는 책.
인류의 이주 역사를 통해 현대 이민 문제에 대한 통찰력 있는 해결책을 제시하고, '이주'가 인간의 본질임을 밝히는 매력적인 역사서. 이 책은 인간이 단순히 전쟁과 빈곤을 피해 떠나는 존재가 아니라, 호기심과 모험심으로 세계를 탐험하는 대담한 여행자임을 생생히 보여준다!

and Korea's 112 emergency reporting system – a phenomenon some call the "Korean wave of security."

Interestingly, the influence of Korean culture extends even to global brands adapting to Korean trends. For instance, KFC launched an ad campaign to leverage the growing global popularity of Korean-style chicken. Korean chicken has gained widespread attention, even in the United States, where the American food magazine "Taste of Home" recognized Korean chicken franchises, such as bb.q Chicken, as the best, and acknowledged Korea as a new hotspot for fried chicken. This has led to the notion of "food born abroad and raised in Korea" to describe how Korean adaptations of foreign foods gain international recognition.

In the content industry, the phenomenon of cultural gradation has become so widespread that nationality is increasingly irrelevant in the creative process. Individuals from various countries, both in front of and behind the camera, collaborate to produce a single piece of content. For example, the Korean film *Broker* was directed by a Japanese filmmaker, the Vietnamese movie *Mai* was produced by a Korean film company, and the joint Korean-Thai drama production *Love is Like a Cat* brought together creators from both nations. Additionally, the Japanese drama *Eye Love You* stars a Korean male actor and a Japanese actress. As Korean content gains global recognition, partnerships between Korean companies and those from other countries are becoming more common, with many signing MOUs to collaborate on future projects.

In fact, this cross-national collaboration extends into major markets. For instance, the popular American drama series *The Good Doctor* includes a notice at the start of each episode stating, "This is a remake of the Korean KBS drama *Good Doctor*." But it's not just dramas; entertainment programs are also exporting their formats. The Korean show *King of Mask Singer*복면가왕 was adapted by FOX in the U.S. as *"The Masked Singer,"* while *Grandpas Over Flowers* was remade as *"Better Late Than Never"* in the U.S. and has been exported to over 10 countries, including the Netherlands and China.

Hwang Jin-woo, CEO of Something Special, a company that exports Korean entertainment formats, stresses that the format business involves transferring key elements such as concepts, planning, program structures, and marketing strategies to ensure local success. The growing global demand for Korean program formats has even led to the emergence of a new term, the "K-format business," highlighting Korea's influence in shaping entertainment across borders.

Market Gradation

The products or services Korean companies sell are largely divided into those for domestic consumption and those for export. In the era of gradation K, this dichotomy is also diversifying. As explained earlier in "People Gradation," as the proportion of foreigners increases, their consumption contexts must also be considered in various ways. This market can be divided into: (1) the market for foreign residents in Korea, (2) the market for tourists visiting Korea, and (3) the market for overseas sales. These are the three aspects of "market gradation," the last type of gradient K.

Market targeting foreign residents in Korea

"I'm no VIP. Is this a voice phishing scam?"

When Hana Bank called to invite its foreign resident customers to the first "VIP foreign worker" event, most respondents were reportedly embarrassed and asked if they were being scammed. Hana Bank selected foreign "VIPs" based on a new criterion of "overseas remittance amount," but foreign residents who did not have a large deposit balance were embarrassed. Recently, the financial industry has been competing fiercely to attract non-Korean customers since reaching a saturation point with attracting domestic customers. In fact, the number of foreign resident customers at the four major banks (KB Kookmin, Shinhan, Hana, and Woori) increased by 15% from 4.13 million in 2019 to 4.79 million in 2023, and 7.7% of Hana Bank's foreign exchange profits came from overseas remittances by foreign workers. Banks are focusing on service convenience as a strategy to preempt foreign resident customers. In order to lower the language barrier, they are launching multilingual services as well as various services that reduce the inconvenience of overseas remittances. The perspective on foreign workers is changing, from being recipients of support to customers.

This phenomenon is not limited to the financial industry. The overall spending power of foreign residents in Korea is rapidly increasing every year. The amount of card payments made by them has increased by 17.03% every year since 2020, reaching 3.7 times the amount of card payments by Korean-born citizens. Along with the increase in spending power itself, the areas of consumption are also diversifying. Unlike the existing consumption that was limited to the basic necessities of food, clothing, and shelter, consumption that improves the quality of life is recently on the rise. Foreign residents are engaging in full-fledged consumption activities such as education for themselves and their children, medical services for a healthy life, and online shopping for general self-care.

This change in consumption is accelerating due to the self-centered tendencies of the younger generations. Unlike the past when people focused on earning foreign currency to support their families in their home countries, young foreign residents have become more inclined to prioritize their own lives, which naturally leads to an increase in their daily consumption. You can also find people pursuing a work-life balance, such as moving away from company-provided dormitories to find comfortable residences and enjoying leisurely weekends rather than working too hard. For foreign residents, Korea, which used to be viewed as just a transit point for making money, is now recognized as a place to live a full, normal life, and foreign residents have emerged as new consumers in the domestic market. In fact, according to analysis by BC Card and GME Remittance, the percentage of foreign workers residing in Korea sending money to their own accounts in their home countries is expected to increase to 20% in 2023 and 25% in 2024. This is a significant change from the past when people would send money to their parents, siblings, and spouses in their home countries without spending a single penny in Korea. They also want to spend their hard-earned money on themselves.

Market targeting tourists visiting Korea

The domestic consumption of tourists visiting Korea is also changing significantly in both quantity and quality. A hair shop in Hongdae area, a personal color diagnosis store in Konkuk University area, and a private bath and sauna in Seongbuk-gu, Seoul. What these three stores have in common is that their clientele are predominantly tourists. As Korea gains new tourism competitiveness based on its cultural content, sales from tourists are showing a high growth rate. In particular, the advancement of the fashion and beauty sectors is remarkable. According to the Tourism Knowledge & Information System, 7 out of 10 tourists visiting Korea in the first half of 2024 visited Olive Young, and the proportion of tourist sales at Olive Young Myeongdong Town Branch exceeded 90%.

Department stores, which are changing to suit the tastes of twenty and thirty-somethings, are also emerging as new must-visit destinations for tourists. As the contribution of tourist sales has increased rapidly, department stores are strengthening exclusive memberships and VIP benefits to attract tourists. They also run beauty classes for visitors who are highly interested in Korean cosmetics. Lotte, Shinsegae, and Hyundai Department Stores all emphasize that the consumption by tourists has changed qualitatively. Unlike the past when it was centered on Chinese group tourists, the number of individual travelers visiting from the US, Europe, Japan, and Southeast Asia has recently increased. A particularly notable change is that interest in Korean brands and street brands has surpassed interest in luxury brands or traditional department store brands. As of March 2024, Hyundai Department Store's top tourist sales brands include Korean beauty and fashion brands Tamburins, Emis, Matin Kim, and Thisisneverthat.

Korea's new designer brands are booming. The so-called "3M" brands – Marithé et François Girbaud, Matin Kim, and Mardi Mercredi, have become must-buy items for tourists visiting Korea. Interest in Korean products, which started with cosmetics, has recently expanded to include fashion brands. Analysis shows that interest in brands among tourists has increased as photos of Korean celebrities with global fans wearing the brands are naturally exposed through social media. In fact, when a photo of Blackpink's Jennie wearing the brand Marithé et François Girbaud was uploaded to social media, the percentage of foreign customers at the brand's Hannam and Hongdae stores increased to over 70%. The interest of tourists can also serve as an indicator of a brand's overseas expansion. In the case of the fashion brand Matin Kim, when the percentage of sales from Japanese tourists exceeded 70% of the monthly sales, they were able to decide to fully advance into the Japanese market.

Day 1: "PC" + Massage – Personal color diagnosis, body
massage
Day 2: Spa Day – Spa, meridian massage
Day 3: Hair Day – Scalp care, hair shop, makeup shop
Day 4: Treatment Day – Beauty clinic, dermatology

If seeing the northern lights is the must-do activity in Iceland, what is the must-do activity in Korea? "Beauty experience" is emerging as a representative itinerary item when visiting Korea. The above 4-day schedule is from a video titled "Beauty Journey in Seoul" by beauty influencer AVA Juwon (@glowwithava), which recorded 380,000 views. It introduces a full beauty experience schedule including personal color diagnosis, spa, meridian massage, and a visit to a beauty clinic. Recently, young tourists have gone beyond simply purchasing products to receiving total beauty care. The tourism trend of preferring experiences over sight-seeing is also apparent among visitors to Korea.

Popular beauty experiences are commonly based on personalized consulting. Rather than a one-time experience, they receive analysis and advice to further upgrade their desired appearance. Dermatologists diagnose the individual's skin condition and characteristics before treatment, and hair shops suggest styles based on the shape of the face. Personal color diagnosis, which only provides analysis and advice, is also popular. As the nationalities of tourists visiting Korea become more diverse, in-store services for tourists are also becoming more diverse. For example, the Hongdae branch of Soonsiki Hair has prepared a private room for tourists who cannot show their hair in public places for religious reasons. And the number of medical tourists visiting Korea in 2023 is expected to exceed 600,000, the highest ever, with some hospitals' tourist sales having surpassed local resident sales.

According to the results of an analysis by Shinhan Card Big Data Research Institute, hospitals ranked third in the consumption sector with the largest spending by tourists, following luxury hotels and department stores. Excluding general hospitals, more than half of clinic payments were for cosmetic purposes, such as plastic surgery or dermatology. In particular, oriental medicine clinics, which showed the highest growth rate among medical departments, are attracting attention. Oriental medicine, which also has a "cultural experience" aspect, is beginning to be recognized as a space for special healing experiences for tourists. As the number of tourists receiving treatment has increased, domestic beauty hospitals such as dermatologists and plastic surgeons are also working hard to improve their services, such as hiring local staff or interpreters and providing one-stop services that support everything from airport pick-ups to hotel accommodations and shopping tours.

Overseas markets that cross borders

As K-food becomes popular overseas, exports of items that are not consumed at all in Korea are also increasing. "K-halal food" is a representative example. Recently, domestic food companies are targeting Muslim markets in Indonesia, the Middle East, and Africa, and are releasing K-halal food products one after another. Samyang Foods, which is most active in exporting K-ramen, was the first domestic ramen company to receive halal certification from the Indonesian Ulema Council in 2017 and is still firmly maintaining its position as the number one halal ramen. Nongshim is exporting products to about 40 countries including Saudi Arabia and Malaysia with "Halal Shin Ramyun," and CJ CheilJedang is also producing about 110 types of halal food, including Bibigo dumplings. The Islamic world, which accounts for 24% of the world's population, is an attractive market, and as K-content is gaining popularity in Indonesia, the world's fourth most populous country, the "halalization" of Korean food has become inevitable.

The case of Miss Darcei, a black beauty creator who directly requested that products developed for Koreans be made available to non-Koreans as well, is also interesting. In a video titled "Darkest Shade of a Korean Foundation," Miss Darcei, who has 3.19 million subscribers, expressed regret over the lack of diverse colors in Korean cosmetics foundations that can be used by consumers with various skin tones. Upon seeing this, TirTir developed a cushion product in 20 colors and gave it to Miss Darcei as a gift, and later released a foundation in 30 colors suitable for every skin tone gradation. As word of mouth spread about K-beauty products that can be used by black people, the product became the first Korean beauty brand to reach #1 in Amazon's Beauty category. It is said that even small fashion brands that sell only to domestic consumers have recently received a significant increase in requests from overseas to have sales reach them.

As more and more brands promote their products based on social media, which is used by consumers all over the world regardless of nationality, the boundaries of product sales are now blurring. In line with this change, Korean brands have recently been responding to the diverse markets that cross borders by providing variations on their products.

Background of the Emergence of Gradation K

The emergence of the gradation K phenomenon can be fundamentally attributed to the increase in global mobility. In particular, individuals worldwide, having been confined to their home countries for nearly three years, are now eager to travel as a means of alleviating their stress. This surge in travel is not merely quantitative; it reflects a shift from a past where individuals were often bound to live their entire lives in their place of birth. People now have the freedom to select their nationality based on personal preferences for various reasons. According to the UN's *World Migration Report 2020*, 3.5% of the global population is engaged in immigration. Countries in Europe and North America, which are often favored destinations for immigrants, have already established themselves as multicultural and multiethnic societies where diverse populations coexist.

Although Korea's immigrant population does not yet match the levels seen in the United States and Europe – where immigrants comprise over 20% of the population – Korea has recently evolved into a multicultural nation. It has transitioned from a nation primarily sending emigrants to one that welcomes immigrants. While the emigration rate for Koreans has been declining, the influx of immigrants into Korea is on the rise. This trend is particularly notable as wages in Korea have rapidly increased in recent years, making it an attractive destination for individuals from low-income countries, especially in Southeast Asia. Additionally, the number of international students is also on the rise; as of April 2024, the Ministry of Education reported that the number of international students studying in Korea exceeded

200,000. This growth is largely a result of universities focusing on attracting international students amid a declining school-age population and frozen tuition fees.

Crucially, Korea's "soft power," or cultural influence, has significantly increased. Films and dramas like *Parasite*, *Squid Game*, *Minari*, and *Pachinko*, alongside K-pop groups such as BTS and Blackpink, have gained global acclaim. Groups like GOT7, SF9, and Dreamcatcher are now more popular in regions like Southeast Asia and South America than in their home country. Consequently, fans are not only flocking to Seoul, the hub of their favorite idol groups, but are also visiting iconic locations featured in K-dramas, including Jeju Island, Namsan, Gyeongbokgung Palace, Seoraksan, and Gyeongju, contributing to a heightened global interest in Korea itself.

The remarkable shift can be attributed to the widespread influence of social media, which has created an environment for the consumption of diverse content without bias. In 2009, Park Jin-young sought to break into the US market with the popular group Wonder Girls, but their efforts fell short of expectations. However, in 2012, PSY's "Gangnam Style" unexpectedly captured global attention. What changed in those three years? The key difference was YouTube. The music video for "Gangnam Style" spread rapidly across the globe via the platform. Since then, services like TikTok, Instagram, and Netflix, which enable simultaneous sharing of content worldwide, have become firmly established. The emergence of these platforms has connected content consumers globally, uniting them through similar tastes. As mentioned in the Preface, unlike Japan, which remained attached to traditional media like CDs, Korean artists who adeptly leveraged these new global platforms for content delivery have been able to achieve worldwide fame.

Today, online memes and challenges have no nationality. Memes from countries few Koreans have ever visited are becoming popular in Korea, and Korean memes are also gaining global recognition. Japan's "Night Dancer," Vietnam's "Ting Ting Tang Tang Tang," India's "Asoka," and China's "Wo Xing Shi" are challenges where people dance to indigenous songs, and they've been hugely popular on TikTok and YouTube. The Korean cheer "Fighting" is actually only used in Korea. In the UK and the US, "Go" or "You've got this!" would be a close equivalent; in China it's "Jjayu"; and in Japan they say "Ganbare." However, "Fighting" has slowly begun to be used in many countries. Son Heung-min is popular not only in Korea and the UK, but also in Southeast Asia and other countries around the world, and fans around the world shout out "Fighting" when cheering for him. It is even said that Korean swear words have become common swear words among global gamers. In Chinese PC rooms, you can often hear Chinese gamers using Korean profanity.

In an online environment where you can get a glimpse of other countries' cultures with just one click or swipe, people around the world live in an environment where they are influenced by people with diverse cultural backgrounds. In this context, it is perhaps inevitable that Korean culture, which has a high relative appeal, is gaining popularity. Now, all things Korean are highly visible on the global stage.

Outlook and Implications

The concept of gradation K has significant implications. First, it is essential to engage with the emerging market of non-Koreans, who are becoming key players in new consumption patterns. Companies that have traditionally focused solely on the domestic Korean market can broaden their perspectives by considering the needs of foreign residents in Korea. Furthermore, there is potential to expand to overseas markets. To achieve these aims, it is crucial to understand and consider the lifestyles of individuals in the target countries. Examples include creating inclusive products, such as make-up foundations with wide-ranging tones, and inclusive environments, such as salons offering private rooms for customers who cannot expose their hair for religious reasons, as well as banks providing weekend services for migrant workers with full-time jobs during the week. Such cultural understanding can greatly aid in attracting new consumers and expanding market reach.

To enhance corporate competitiveness, building an infrastructure that allows overseas experts to showcase their talents is imperative. The *Wall Street Journal* has cited the increased influx of immigrants as a key factor driving the robust recovery of the US economy after COVID-19. The expansion of the labor force due to immigration has suppressed inflation and bolstered economic growth and fiscal expansion in the United States. Similarly, the International Monetary Fund has found that a 1% increase in the percentage of immigrants among employed individuals in advanced countries correlates with a 1% rise in GDP after five years. The enhanced productivity attributed to immigrants results in higher average incomes for local populations.

To foster such positive outcomes, efforts must be made to attract skilled human resources from abroad. Currently, the proportion of professional talent among foreign resident workers in Korea stands at only 13.7%, a relatively low figure compared to other nations. In addition to addressing existing skill shortages, there is a pressing need to increase the number of professionals suited for the era of technological dominance. As countries evolve into destinations for immigrants, we must advance further by establishing a system that attracts top-tier human resources from overseas.

A more profound question arises: what does it mean to be "Korean" in the era of gradation K? The identity of Korea as we know it is at a pivotal juncture. Koreans, Korean culture, and Korean society are all undergoing transformation. As these changes unfold, our understanding of what is "Korean" must also evolve. A few years ago, the inclusion into the Oxford English Dictionary of numerous Korean words like "oppa" and "mukbang" sparked significant discussion. The Oxford English Dictionary, adhering to strict "historical principles," does not dictate how words should be used but rather reflects their usage over time, continuously revising and adding entries to create a dynamic representation of English. In contrast, the Standard Korean Dictionary has yet to incorporate commonly used terms among Koreans, such as "KakaoTalk," "Zoom," "chicken and beer치맥," or even "mukbang."

This is not merely an issue of dictionary entries. The Oxford Dictionary's actions signify the direction Korea must take in the gradation K era. What it means to be "Korean" in this context is not rooted in a stagnant past but is reflected in the everyday lives of contemporary Koreans. Have we been overly fixated on tradition and authenticity regarding Korean culture? Changes in trends necessitate shifts in our thinking. If the gradation K trend is an unstoppable force that offers a positive outlook for South Korea amid declining population challenges, embracing an open mindset becomes essential. It is now up to us to determine how receptive we can be to the world. Our non-Korean brothers and sisters should be seen not merely as resources but as neighbors.

- Korea is now a multicultural country.
- A girl group with all foreign members —is it truly
  K-pop?
- What truly defines being Korean?

E

Experiencing the Physical:
the Appeal of Materiality

In a world dominated by digital information, there's still something uniquely powerful about what we can touch and feel. Even in this "immaterial age," we still crave tangible experiences. This power – the ability to make something physically real and compelling – is known as "materiality appeal."

Take the growing trend of "content materialization," where characters and worlds from animations and dramas are brought to life in physical spaces. As brands place more emphasis on their values and lifestyles, we're seeing a rise in brand materialization, where companies offer consumers a chance to experience the brand in a tangible way. Likewise, technological advancements, like robots recreating physical objects, are another form of materialization.

As digital and virtual experiences grow, the desire for something real becomes stronger. Despite the world's rapid shift to digital and virtual realms, the human need for physical, sensory experiences isn't going anywhere anytime soon. The gap between our sensory instincts and the efficiency of digital virtualization only heightens this appeal. Consumers increasingly yearn for the authentic touch and feel of real objects. It's about making those sensations come alive.

Imagine you're in charge of marketing a movie this year that your company is extremely excited about. The film is well made, but with declining movie attendance, the pressure mounts. What would you do? First, you'd likely create multiple versions of a sleek poster, plastering it on buses, taxis, subways – anywhere to catch people's eyes. You'd launch big ad campaigns across TV, newspapers, radio, and movie magazines. On social media, you'd collaborate with influencers to make the film go viral on platforms like YouTube, Instagram, X, Facebook, and Kakao Page. But could there be a better way?

Consider Disney's unique approach with *Inside Out 2* in June 2024. They opened a pop-up store in a department store in Seoul right before the release. A pop-up store for a movie? Instead of just posters or character dolls, the standout attraction was the "Thought Train." This train, which the movie's characters use to navigate Riley's mind, was recreated in the store, allowing visitors to feel like they were stepping into the animated world. After the ride, participants could store "memory beads," mimicking the film's emotional journey. This immersive experience let the audience engage with the movie's characters and props in a tangible way before even entering the theater.

Today's audiences aren't content with just watching a movie – they want to touch, own, and experience the story. To meet these demands, the trend is to transfer the narrative from the screen to the real world. While goods and photo zones are standard, the key is to create experiences that make the movie's world come alive. In today's market, content must leap off the screen and into the audience's hands to truly captivate and draw them in.

And it's not just movies – many industries are increasingly giving consumers physical experiences to engage their senses. This concept is known as "materiality," and we would like to call the ability to enhance a product's appeal by making it tangibly experiential "materiality appeal." "Materiality" refers to the inherent properties of a substance, meaning only physical materials can possess it. This makes it challenging to convey the materiality of intangible elements like brands, technologies, and organizational cultures, including content such as movies. Materiality appeal involves creating cognitive, emotional, and behavioral experiences by engaging all available senses – sight, touch, hearing, smell, and taste – so consumers can truly feel these properties. In essence, materiality appeal is about making consumers aware (cognitively), attracted (emotionally), and com-pelled to purchase (behaviorally) through tangible experiences.

So, why is materiality appeal set to become crucial in the 2025 market? It's largely due to the increasing need for consumer experiences. As new technologies rapidly emerge, introducing unprecedented services with innovative concepts, it's often difficult for consumers to adapt. To help them understand these new services, offering a physical experience that directly demonstrates their benefits is key – this is best achieved through materiality rather than abstract explanations. Additionally, prolonged COVID-19 quarantines and the rise of the contactless economy have limited the number of sensory experiences available to people, intensifying their desire for tangible interactions. The more the economy becomes virtual, the stronger the demand for materiality becomes. In this experience-driven market, the most important trend in recent marketing is how effectively and realistically materiality appeal can be delivered to consumers.

Children instinctively touch and even taste objects, regardless of potential dangers, illustrating the innate human desire for materiality. Homo sapiens has walked, run, and danced for nearly 10,000 years, but has only recently encountered the virtual world. Which is more essential? Materiality appeal represents a return to the fundamental human longing for the physical in a modern society dominated by the digital and AI. As digital, virtual, and contactless economies continue to grow, the importance of materiality appeal will only increase.

Various Aspects of Materialization

Phenomenon 1. Materialization of content

The hottest trend in the K-pop industry right now is "virtual idols," and leading this wave is PLAVE. This 4th generation male idol group has captivated Gen Z, breaking records with their second mini-album, which sold 570,000 copies in its first week in February 2024. They topped the music charts on *Show! Music Core*쇼! 음악중심 in March 2024 and made history by joining Melon's "Billions Club" in record time, achieving 1 billion streams across all their songs.

However, PLAVE faces a unique challenge: as virtual idols, they lack a physical presence. How can fans connect more deeply with these screen-bound characters? This is where the power of materiality comes into play. To celebrate the release of their second album *ASTERUM: 134-1* in March 2024, PLAVE launched a pop-up store. The highlight was the "Proto Hologram" booth, which used real-time hologram technology to allow fans to take photos or videos with a holographic member of PLAVE. The response was overwhelming – fans were thrilled by the rare chance to interact with their favorite virtual idols in a tangible way. This experience brought the virtual characters to life, bridging the gap between the digital and physical worlds. The pop-up store drew over 20,000 visitors eager to see PLAVE in this groundbreaking format.

Theme parks are designed to offer an escape from daily life, where visitors can focus solely on enjoying memorable experiences. For years, ways to create more realistic and immersive experiences have been explored. Recently, Everland has taken this to the next level by materializing content, going beyond traditional landscaping and rides. A prime example is Everland's "Blood City," an immersive horror experience designed to evoke fear. Known as the ultimate Halloween destination, Blood City introduces a new story every fall, delivered with sensory intensity.

In the fall of 2024, Everland partnered with Netflix to thematically tie Blood City to popular shows like *All of Us Are Dead* and *Stranger Things*. This collaboration has generated high expectations among Netflix fans, who are excited to see, hear, touch, and even smell the narratives they've only experienced on screen, brought to life in Everland's iconic spaces.

There's a growing trend of closely linking content with the physical characteristics of a space to enhance the appeal of its material properties. A notable example is Nintendo's *Animal Crossing: New Horizons*, which chose COEX Aquarium as a venue for a unique consumer experience, sparking excitement among fans. The aquarium allowed visitors to encounter real marine life featured in the game, while various themed goods and experience zones, like taking photos with *Animal Crossing* characters placed throughout the space, heightened the sense of immersion.

One of the most praised aspects was the game's background

music (BGM) playing continuously throughout the aquarium. For Gen Z, *Animal Crossing's* BGM is synonymous with "peace," and hearing it while exploring the aquarium created a vivid sensation, making visitors feel as though they were truly inside the game. This collaboration underscored the importance of choosing a space that aligns with the content's world to create a tangible, immersive experience.

Phenomenon 2. Materialization of brands

It's now widely recognized that a brand's philosophy and story are crucial. Consumers increasingly want to connect with a brand's narrative, not just its products. As a result, efforts to translate a brand's intangible values into physical experiences that engage the five senses have become essential. Recently, brands have been using a variety of physical mediums – such as pop-up stores, media art, cultural spaces, and branded goods – to convey their stories.

One standout example from the winter of 2023 was the "Flop Sunyang Pop-up Store" in Seongsu-dong, Seoul, which captured the attention of Gen Z. The soju brand Sunyang선양소주 created this pop-up under the theme "A journey to meet a whale who fell in love with Sunyang Soju." During its three-week run, the store attracted 17,800 visitors and garnered over 20,000 Likes on social media. The highlight of the pop-up was the "artificial sea" zone, where visitors could ride a boat shaped like a bottle cap across a water-filled space. Unlike typical water-themed displays, which usually feature small puddles, this pop-up filled an entire area with water, allowing for an immersive boating experience that amazed visitors. The event concluded with a simple game, where participants could win a taste of Sunyang Soju paired with *oden*. By the end of the experience, it seemed that it wasn't just the whales, but the visitors themselves who had fallen in love with Sunyang Soju.

Media art is also being utilized to bring invisible concepts to life in a more immersive way. In January 2024, the cosmetics brand MISSHA transformed its Myeongdong Megastore into an experiential space themed around "Ganghwa Island." The story involved visitors seeking a hidden secret on the island to soothe their troubled skin. Through media art, the journey simulated the clear sea, sea breeze, mineral-rich soil, and sunlight of Ganghwa Island. The experience culminated in a "True World" zone, where the temperature was deliberately warmer, symbolizing the successful completion of the journey and the calming of the skin. This is a prime example of how a brand can "sensorialize" its message through both physical and environmental cues.

Brands are increasingly expanding their reach by creating permanent cultural spaces that embody their values, moving beyond the short-lived pop-up model. One such example is "Noir Mardi Mercredi," a complex cultural space launched in April 2024 by the online fashion brand Mardi Mercredi. CEO Park Hwa-mok described the venture as an extension of the brand's original ethos, stating, "I thought it was cool that a company ignored the goal of making money and still made money without the intention to do so." The space reflects Mardi Mercredi's founding principle: to prioritize cool, authentic experiences over commercial gain. Noir Mardi Mercredi, which features a café, a living "select shop셀렉트샵," and a record shop, draws 400-500 visitors on weekdays and 700-800 on weekends, all eager to immerse themselves in the brand's philosophy.

Similarly, "Simmon's Terrace," operated by mattress manufacture Simmons시몬스, offers consumers a multi-sensory brand experience. Located in Icheon, Gyeonggi Province, this complex cultural space includes exhibitions, food and beverage outlets, cultural events, museums, and showrooms. One of its standout features is a farmer's market where local Icheon farmers sell their produce. This market physically embodies Simmons' brand goal of fostering regional connections and socializing – a theme central to their identity. Thanks to these initiatives, Simmon's Terrace has welcomed over 1 million visitors within five years of its opening, earning the distinction of being the most visited complex cultural space in the Seoul Metropolitan Area according to the navigation app T Map.

Brand materialization proves especially valuable in industries where direct consumer interaction with products is limited, such as finance. The fintech company Toss토스 has creatively tackled this challenge, given that it lacks physical storefronts. One notable effort was the production of a documentary in 2021, which captured the essence of the fintech industry from Toss's perspective, highlighting its working methods and organizational culture to convey the brand's message through content.

In May 2024, Toss took another step in this direction by publishing *The Money Book*, a comprehensive guide to managing one's financial life. The book quickly became a bestseller, reflecting its popularity. Toss further engaged consumers by participating in the 2024 Seoul International Book Fair, where attendees could create their own "Money Book" at the Toss booth, offering an indirect yet meaningful experience of the brand's philosophy.

Similarly, the household detergent brand Yuhanrox유한락스 found success with its 2022 publication, *The White Book*. This book, filled with questions and answers about their product and accurate cleaning tips, received positive feedback. Consumers often keep this brand book handy, using it as a reference for cleaning, which naturally deepens their connection to the brand over time. These examples demonstrate how brand materialization can effectively engage consumers in sectors where traditional product experiences are less feasible.

Phenomenon 3. Materialization of technology

Many companies are increasingly investing in new technologies, including artificial intelligence. However, possessing advanced technological capabilities and translating those capabilities into tangible experiences are two distinct challenges. It is crucial for companies to transform abstract concepts into functional products that allow consumers to experience their utility firsthand. Materializing technology helps consumers understand and appreciate its benefits on a personal level.

In Jincheon County, North Chungcheong Province, three unique modular houses – labeled "the beneficial house," "the small house," and "the communicative house" – were installed for the *House Vision* exhibition focusing on future rural living. These houses can be reserved for overnight stays, providing guests with a hands-on experience. Notably, the beneficial house, also known as the "Smart Cottage," was developed in collaboration with LG Electronics and GS E&C. This 31.4 square meter duplex structure integrates LG's smart home solutions, showcasing energy-related technologies that might otherwise go unnoticed. It features a roof equipped with photovoltaic (PV) panels, an air-to-water heat pump (AWHP), an energy storage system (ESS), and a power conditioning system (PCS). Any surplus electricity generated can be sold to electric utility KEPCO or used to charge electric vehicles. This setup allows guests to physically engage with the technology and appreciate its benefits, even if they are unfamiliar with technical terms like PV, AWHP, ESS, or PCS.

AI-driven firms in the current IT and electronics landscape have chosen robotics as a medium to materialize AI's advantages. At CES 2024, a showcase of cutting-edge robotics took center stage, particularly with Samsung Electronics and LG Electronics unveiling their latest AI butler robots. Samsung introduced its second-generation AI butler, "Bollie," which autonomously navigates the home, assists with household tasks via a secondary screen, and tracks exercise routines. This development moves it closer to commercialization as a practical AI assistant. Meanwhile, LG unveiled "Q9," a smart home AI agent that enhances user interaction through a display capable of various facial expressions. This adds an emotional layer to the functional utility of an AI butler, enriching the consumer experience. Goldman Sachs predicts that by 2035, over 1 million consumer humanoid robots will be produced annually. As AI technology advances and the cost of production declines, we can expect to see AI increasingly take physical form through robotics in the near future.

Phenomenon 4. Materialization of corporate organizational culture

"You can know a company by looking at its workspace."

Every organization embodies its founder's philosophy and unique culture, often articulated through a company motto or CEO message. When the workplace reflects these principles, it becomes easier for employees to internalize the organization's values. Recently, many companies have emphasized design and interior aesthetics that align with their core philosophies when constructing headquarters. Beyond the physical spaces, organizations are also exploring ways to convey their culture through branded goods tailored for employees. While this may resemble brand materialization, it distinctly targets the organization's members rather than customers.

The entertainment industry exemplifies how headquarters can embody organizational culture. In 2023, Hive established its Yongsan headquarters with an emphasis on the core values of connection, expansion, and relationships. Recognizing the industry's reliance on creativity and inspiration, Hive opted for a design that forgoes traditional finishing materials and standard office layouts in favor of adjustable workspaces that foster creativity and free-thinking.

Similarly, JYP recently gained attention by selecting a design proposal from Hyunjoon Yoo Architects유현준 건축사사무소 for its new building. The concept, titled "BAPSANG밥상," references a traditional Korean family dining table where members gather to share meals. This design approach seeks to harmonize the diverse personalities of its artists and office staff, encouraging interaction and communication as if they were sharing a meal together. Additionally, the design will integrate natural elements within the building, promoting a sense of well-being akin to enjoying healthy food. As JYP moves forward with this concept, all eyes are on how effectively the company will translate its goals into the physical space.

Hyundai Engineering & Construction has taken a unique approach to embody its organizational philosophy through apparel. Partnering with workwear brand Boldest볼디스트, the company

- People want to see and touch.
- How can we give digital things physical properties?
- Analog materiality is becoming increasingly rare.

created a special edition "MA-1 padded jumper" exclusively for its employees. Traditionally, workwear referred to clothing designed for manual laborers, but it has recently evolved into a trendy fashion statement. This new iteration allows for customization, featuring Velcro patches where employees can attach and detach company insignia, team logos, and personal decorations. This flexibility caters to the tastes of Gen MZ, who appreciate the option to wear the jumper outside of work and personalize it to their liking.

The initiative proved highly successful, with nearly 6,000 jumpers sold within a short 10-day period. Orders came from over 140 domestic and international locations, and 1,200 pieces were purchased individually. Beyond this, Hyundai Engineering & Construction continues to innovate with branded merchandise. They are collaborating with casual street brand Covernat커버낫 to produce hooded zip-ups and developing camping gear with outdoor brands Helinox and Nalgene. These efforts reflect the company's desire to move away from a traditionally conservative corporate culture and embrace a more youthful, dynamic identity through its clothing and merchandise.

Materiality Gains Importance Amid Digital Dominance

In his book *Undinge: Umbrüche der Lebenswelt (Non-things:*

Upheaval in the Lifeworld), philosopher Byung-chul Han한병철 explores a shift from a focus on physical objects to an emphasis on reflections and information in our digital age. Han argues that the digital order has transformed the world into a realm defined by information rather than tangible objects. Yet, in this era where virtual realities increasingly shape our existence and technology surpasses human capabilities, why is materiality gaining renewed significance?

Culture reporter Kim Seong-hyeon of the *Chosun Ilbo* highlights a curious trend in a recent column. Despite the rise of a generation that is reading less and the book industry's decline, the 2024 Seoul International Book Fair drew an impressive 150,000 attendees. Similarly, despite claims that rock music is dead, young people continue to flock to rock festivals. Classical music, often declared obsolete, still sells out concerts by artists like Seong-jin Cho and Yunchan Lim within seconds. Kim attributes these phenomena to a shift where "consumers are leading more than suppliers, transitioning from ownership to experience." This growing appetite for tangible experiences is particularly pronounced in the information age, saturated with digital interactions and AI.

A prominent example of this shift is the resurgence of vinyl records. According to the Shinhan Card Big Data Research Institute, visits to offline LP-related venues – such as LP shops, cafés, and bars – increased by approximately 54% in 2024 compared to the previous year. Notably, people in their 20s are driving this trend, using LPs not only for music but also for decoration and collecting. This trend underscores a paradox in a digitally dominated era: the rising allure of physical, hands-on experiences.

The role of branding is undergoing a significant transformation. Traditionally, brands were crafted with a focus on differentiation and identity, conveyed through mass media like TV and radio. Branding involved creating visual and conceptual elements such as logos, packaging, slogans, and names. However, with the rise of interactive media – such as social media and YouTube – branding is evolving to create deeper, more subjective connections with consumers. This modern approach, known as "brand experience (BX)," emphasizes the engagement of consumers through tangible and sensory interactions. Today, a brand is increasingly defined by the overall experience it offers, necessitating the physical embodiment of its abstract concepts, technology, and organizational culture.

Moreover, as technological change accelerates, consumers face a constant barrage of new products and innovations, leaving them with limited time to grasp their utility. For instance, while the metaverse was a major buzzword just a few years ago, its prominence has waned, giving way to the rapidly advancing field of AI. According to a recent Stanford University report, AI's performance improvement has outpaced Moore's Law by a factor of seven, highlighting the rapid evolution of this technology. Despite the flood of technical terms like "AGI" and "LLM" in the media, understanding and experiencing AI remains challenging.

Experts anticipate that AI's appeal will persist due to its clear utility compared to the metaverse. Multimodal interfaces, which allow AI to interact through speech, visual displays, and tactile feedback, are expected to enhance consumer engagement. However, for AI to achieve widespread market adoption, it must be perceived as useful by the general public. Companies face the critical task of demonstrating the practical value of these new technologies. Even the most advanced innovations will fall short if they fail to resonate with consumers and meet their needs. As a result, the tangible aspects of products and services are becoming increasingly significant in bridging the gap between cutting-edge technology and consumer experience.

Outlook and Implications

Religion may offer the most profound insights into the significance of materiality. To convey the presence of an invisible deity and foster belief, religious traditions construct physical spaces like temples, create sacred images, and adhere to detailed rituals. The Bible reflects this principle with the passage, "In the beginning was the Word..." (John 1:1), establishing the importance of the "Word" as the origin of all things, as well as its "incarnation" with the phrase, "And the Word became flesh..." (John 1:14). Incarnation represents the process through which the sacred is made tangible.

In religious practice, the experience of entering a grand sanctuary, performing rituals before realistic depictions of divinity, and engaging with religious materiality can profoundly deepen faith. Can we envision Islam without mosques or Buddhism without statues? The significance of materiality in these traditions highlights its essential role. As we look ahead, how might the appeal of materiality evolve?

First, it's important to recognize that materialization doesn't have to be grand or complex. Simple items like cotton towels, mugs, and pencils, though seemingly trivial, can significantly foster consumer loyalty by conveying a brand's sincerity. Material appeal doesn't always require elaborate technology or high production values; even a single pencil or cup can effectively represent a brand.

Second, while materialization has traditionally relied on tangible, touch-based interactions, it is anticipated to evolve into a multi-sensory experience encompassing all five senses. A prime example is the pop-up event by the plant care brand "Sunday Planet선데이플래닛47" for Arbor Day in 2023. One of its experience zones allowed visitors to engage with plants through all five senses. Participants could smell plant scents, hear the unique wavelengths of plants converted into sound, and taste various plant flavors. Space researchers suggest that our identity is shaped by the layered experiences and environments we encounter. In the commercial realm, materialized spaces that engage touch, sound, and smell can create positive brand associations.

Looking forward, it is likely that experience design will increasingly integrate all five senses to enhance consumer engagement.

"The post office will deliver pocket money to your parents!"

Korea Post has launched a unique service that delivers pocket money directly to parents in their hometowns. While bank transfers are convenient and free, Korea Post's service emphasizes the emotional impact of receiving physical cash rather than just seeing a deposit in a bank account. The tangible nature of receiving an envelope with money is intended to convey a child's regret for not being able to visit in person during *Chuseok* (the mid-autumn harvest festival), highlighting how materiality can move hearts more profoundly than virtual interactions.

The difference between money as a digital number and as physical cash is significant. In the U.S., for instance, tipping practices reveal this contrast. Research shows that people who tip with a credit card tend to leave 13% more than those who tip with cash. Additionally, purchases made with credit cards are often decided upon more quickly compared to cash transactions. When physical money is not felt, people tend to spend more freely and in greater amounts.

This preference for physical items extends to other areas of life. At amusement parks or museums, visitors often purchase souvenirs to "materialize" their experiences. Similarly, some people buy gold nuggets despite the added tax, reflecting a desire to hold onto tangible symbols of their savings. Despite the rapid digitization of the world, the human inclination towards physical, analog experiences persists. As the efficiency of digital interactions continues to evolve, the appeal of materiality will likely become even more pronounced. Consumers today increasingly seek to reconnect with the tangible sensations of the material world.

Need for
Climate Sensitivity

기후감수성

"The era of global warming has ended; the era of global boiling has arrived." Every year, we face unprecedented climate change and disasters that previously occurred only once in a decade. Climate change is no longer a future threat that might happen someday; it is an "existing danger" that demands immediate action. "Climate sensitivity" – the proactive response to climate issues and the active implementation of solutions – has become an essential virtue for surviving on a rapidly heating planet that is dramatically changing our lives. Climate sensitivity is becoming increasingly important across all sectors, including (1) consumption, (2) business, and (3) public policy.

"Weather insurance" is emerging, and "climate welfare" for vulnerable populations is becoming increasingly vital. Until now, we have often viewed abnormal climate events as "someone else's problem," affecting polar bears in the Arctic or the people of Tuvalu in the Pacific – an exceptional, "over there" phenomenon. However, as terms like "water bomb" and "scorching heat" become part of everyday language each summer, we are reminded that climate issues are now a constant presence. Climate sensitivity is no longer a choice; it is an essential task for survival on a boiling Earth.

July 22, 2024:

Planet's Hottest Day on Record Broken in Just One Day

On July 21, 2024, the World Meteorological Organization announced that the hottest day in Earth's history had been recorded. The Earth's surface temperature averaged 17.09°C, the highest since climate observations began in 1940. Remarkably, less than 24 hours after that announcement, a new record was set with a temperature of 17.15°C. In just one day, a new heat record was established, marking July 22, 2024, as the hottest day in Earth's observational history. Today, we are experiencing unprecedented weather anomalies that used to happen once in a decade, now occurring every year – or even every day.

As records of extreme events like once-in-a-millennia floods, once-in-a-century heatwaves and heavy snowfalls are repeated each season, people are increasingly recognizing the climate crisis as a problem that affects daily life. What was once an invisible threat has now become a real danger that demands immediate resolution, fundamentally altering our routines. In response, the importance of not only mitigating climate change by reducing greenhouse gases but also adapting to the changes that have already occurred is becoming clear.

"Climate adaptation," which involves rapid responses to minimize damage from extreme weather events, is emerging as a key survival strategy. People who are particularly attuned to changes in their environment are often described as "sensitive." In this context, "sensitivity" refers to the capacity of an organism or sense organ to respond to stimulation. Among the various stimuli we encounter in the external world, the most striking and impactful have come from the recent climate crisis.

Given this, we propose the term "climate sensitivity" to describe the ability to quickly perceive and respond to changes in the environment brought about by the climate crisis. Let's explore how people today are adapting to the relentless rise in global temperatures.

Climate Sensitivity: The Ability to Survive a Boiling Planet

In July 2023, the UN declared the end of the global warming era, marking the beginning of the "boiling era" While the climate has always been in flux, this shift is unprecedented in its speed and impact. Throughout history, climate change has been a constant force, shaping the evolution and survival of countless species.

During the Paleozoic and Mesozoic eras, and even into the Cenozoic era, which began 66 million years ago, changes in climate have caused the rise and fall of many species, including humans.

The climate change we face today is alarming not only because of its severity but also because of its drastically shortened cycle. According to the Intergovernmental Panel on Climate Change (IPCC), the average global temperature has risen by 0.6°C in just the past 100 years. This is an unprecedented increase – greater than any seen in the last 10,000 years since the advent of agriculture. *The IPCC's Sixth Assessment Report*, often referred to as the "Global Climate Change Diagnosis," warns that the window of opportunity to avert catastrophe is rapidly closing. If greenhouse gas emissions do not begin to decline after peaking in 2025, the chance to prevent further damage will slip away.

Rising temperatures are only part of the problem. Recent climate change is fundamentally altering the way we live and, perhaps most critically, is directly impacting the global economy. The yields of key crops like coffee, sugar, and cocoa have plummeted, leading to skyrocketing prices and the coining of the term "climate inflation." In the restaurant industry, it's becoming increasingly common for certain menu items to disappear due to the unstable supply of raw ingredients caused by sudden heavy rains. The economic consequences of climate crises such as torrential rains and snowstorms are worsening, with global economic losses estimated at approximately 330 trillion won last year alone.

To navigate and survive the escalating climate disaster, developing climate sensitivity is more crucial than ever. This emerging trend reflects the struggles of people adapting to life in the new era of a boiling planet. Climate sensitivity – actively responding to climate change and taking proactive steps to address it – has become an essential virtue for thriving on a hotter planet.

Let's explore how three sectors – consumption, business, and public policy – are adapting to and addressing the challenges posed by climate change.

Living in the Age of Climate Sensitivity

Consumer life changed by the weather

"Hey Czechia, what's the weather like in Seoul today?"

As sudden and extreme weather changes become more frequent, the number of people turning to foreign weather forecast apps is skyrocketing. These so-called "weather exiles" are seeking more reliable forecasts from sites like the Czech Republic's windy.com, the US-based AccuWeather, and Norway's YR. According to Mobile Index, in July 2024, the number of monthly active users of windy.com in South Korea reached 850,000 – an increase of about 34% from the previous month. This figure even surpassed the user base of all Korean weather apps.

The rise in weather exiles reflects growing dissatisfaction with local forecasts, which often miss the mark due to increasingly unpredictable weather patterns. But more than that, it highlights the deep anxiety and fatigue people are experiencing because of rapid and erratic climate shifts. Extreme weather events have driven people to seek more accurate weather apps, highlighting how quickly we are experiencing the effects of climate change.

The effects of the climate crisis are becoming increasingly visible in our everyday lives, even at the dinner table. Fruits that were once exclusive to Southeast Asia – such as papaya, cherries, and passion fruit – are now being grown domestically in South Korea, transforming them into local produce. In Yanggu County of Gangwon Province, where tropical plant cultivation was once unthinkable due to its high latitude and cold weather, farmers have even begun to grow melons. This drastic shift in the fruit map of the Korean Peninsula is a direct result of the rapidly warming climate.

Apple cultivation, long a hallmark of Korean agriculture, is steadily moving northward as well due to rising temperatures. These apples, now often referred to as "golden apples," are becoming increasingly rare in their traditional growing areas. But the changes don't stop with fruit. The warming waters of the East Sea have led to a significant decline in squid populations, once a staple catch. Swarms of jellyfish now plague these waters, while the squid catch has plummeted, making squid a rare delicacy. In fact, between January and November of last year, South Korea's domestic squid catch was less than 60,000 tons – down from 250,000 tons in 2013, a staggering drop of over 75% in just a decade. In response to these dramatic changes, the fishing industry is looking for alternative fishing grounds, with Kenya emerging as a potential new source.

As weather patterns shift, so too does fashion, adapting to the new climate realities. In South Korea, the "rainy look" has surged in popularity, becoming an everyday style choice due to the persistent heavy rains that continue even beyond the traditional rainy season. Fashion platforms like Zigzag지그재그 and Ably에이블리 reported a dramatic increase in searches for "rainy season look" in May, with jumps of 2,819% and 530%, respectively, compared to the same period last year.

Traditionally, the "rainy look" was all about functionality – think raincoats and boots designed to keep the rain out. However, recent trends are moving beyond mere practicality, emphasizing versatile styling options that can be worn regardless of the weather. For instance, boots that function as rain boots during wet weather and as regular boots when it's dry are gaining traction. Additionally, hybrid items like bags that double as windbreakers are becoming increasingly popular.

The phenomenon of the "goblin rainy season도깨비 장마," where torrential downpours are followed by bright sunshine within minutes, has also led to a rise in demand for special umbrellas that can serve as both umbrellas and parasols. This shift has even influenced cultural norms, with more men in Korea carrying parasols on the streets. The expanding variety of umbrella designs and types has helped to break the stereotype that parasols are exclusively for women, reflecting how fashion is evolving in response to the unpredictable weather patterns of our time.

The travel industry is also adapting to the new realities of climate change, showing a significant shift in both airborne safety concerns and destination preferences. Unpredictable and increasingly frequent episodes of acute turbulence are becoming a major issue for air travel. According to the Ministry of Land, Infrastructure and Transport, domestic aircraft encountered approximately 6,000 instances of turbulence in the first quarter of this year alone – an 80% increase from the previous year. Viral videos capturing the chaos caused by turbulence have heightened public awareness, prompting the airline industry to take proactive measures. For example, Korean Air has adjusted its in-flight services by ending cabin service earlier for safety reasons and discontinuing the serving of hot cup noodles in economy class, where seats are closer to one another. Experts predict that air turbulence will only become more severe in the future, leading the government to explore further countermeasures.

Climate change is also reshaping travel destinations. Traditional tropical beach resorts are losing their appeal due to extreme heatwaves, while "coolcations" (cool + vacation) are gaining popularity. Northern European countries like Finland, Norway, and Iceland, once overlooked due to their cold and dark climates, are now being re-evaluated as attractive vacation spots with stunning scenery. According to Kensington Tours, a global travel agency, reservations for Finland from June to August 2024 increased by 126% compared to the previous year, with Sweden and Norway also seeing significant increases of 70% and 37%, respectively.

Closer to home, Sapporo, Japan, is emerging as a popular coolcation destination. Traditionally known for its winter tourism thanks to its famous snowy landscapes, Sapporo has seen a surge in summer visitors. Travel platform Yeogi Eottae여기어때 reported that the number of accommodations booked in Sapporo from July to August 2024 increased by 2.7 times compared to the same period last year, surpassing even popular Japanese cities like Osaka and Tokyo. This shift in travel patterns highlights the growing desire for cooler climates as people adapt to the challenges posed by global warming.

Climate even affects our emotions beyond our consumer lifestyles. Other than simply feeling hot or cold, the number of people suffering from "climate depression" is increasing, which involves fundamental concerns such as "How should we live under such extreme climates in the future?" Climate depression is a type of depressive disorder defined by the American Psychological Association, and the number of people suffering it has been increasing in Korea recently. According to a recent national environmental awareness survey conducted by the Korea Environmental Institute, when hearing about the seriousness of climate change, 83.1% of respondents said, "I feel anxious because I don't know what kind of disaster or threat will occur in the future," 55.7% said, "I feel sorry for leaving a bad environment for future generations," and 42.9% said, "I feel helpless because my personal efforts are not helpful in solving climate change." This shows that people are experiencing various negative emotions as they face the climate crisis in their daily lives.

The rising climate business

When consumption changes, so does business. Companies are more sensitive to the impact of the climate crisis. Sudden weather changes can directly affect the supply of raw materials and completely change consumers' purchasing behavior. Accordingly, companies have recently begun to explore "climate business" based on climate sensitivity. Beyond efforts to protect the environment, such as reducing carbon emissions, the number of companies that present smart climate solutions that solve problems caused by abnormal climate is on the rise.

The changes in the construction and interior design industries are immediately noticeable. In recent years, as energy prices have risen sharply, "high-insulation windows" that reduce heating and cooling costs have become popular. For example, Kumho Petrochemical's Hugreen휴그린 attracted much attention by introducing their "Automatic Ventilation Window Pro자동환기창 Pro," which automatically ventilates without opening the window using AI smart functions. Opening windows for ventilation when the outside weather is hot or cold results in energy waste, but the high-performance triple-filter system allows ventilation without opening the window, maintaining a constant indoor temperature. In a similar vein, there's the energy-efficiency standard known as "passive house," which refers to an innovative house that blocks direct inflow of outside air and maintains warmth and coolness for a long time. In Korea, where most houses are apartments, construction examples are emerging one after another and are being introduced as a form of housing suitable in the era of climate crisis.

Meanwhile, in the United States, "dome homes" designed to withstand hurricanes are gaining attention. The *New York Times* described them as "disaster-proof homes," noting, "as weather grows more extreme, geodesic domes and other resilient home designs are gaining new attention from more climate-conscious home buyers, and the architects and builders who cater to them." One of those builders – Geoship – constructs dome homes with bioceramic materials capable of withstanding temperatures up to 1,260 degrees Celsius. These homes are also wind-resistant and keep interiors cool during heat waves by using exterior materials that reflect 80% of solar heat.

The automobile industry is also actively introducing solutions to address extreme weather that threatens consumer safety. Volvo has unveiled an "interior radar" system designed to prevent heatstroke or hypothermia if someone is trapped inside a vehicle. This system automatically activates the air conditioning to maintain a comfortable temperature when it detects movement in a locked car. Hyundai Motor Company has garnered attention with its development of a "nano cooling film" that reduces interior vehicle temperatures by over 10°C in the summer. Unlike traditional films, it allows for adjustable transparency, making it legal in countries like Pakistan where tinting is restricted. This technology was also applied to the "radiant energy cooling cap복사냉각 모자" used by Team Korea's archers, in association with Kolon, contributing to their strong performance at the 2024 Paris Olympics, which were reportedly the hottest Games on record. Additionally, Samsung Electro-Mechanics announced plans to mass-produce by the end of the year automotive camera modules that can function reliably in snowy or frozen conditions. These modules feature a heated lens that can melt snow or frost within a minute. Various technologies are being developed to ensure safe autonomous driving even in harsh weather conditions.

In the agriculture and food sectors, which are directly impacted by climate change, there is a growing trend to bolster food security through food tech. This involves creating "super crop varieties" that can withstand extreme weather and developing alternative foods that mimic the taste and nutrition of traditional foods.

As abnormal weather events become more frequent, demand for insurance products is also rising, particularly for "weather insurance" that protects against unpredictable changes in climate. For instance, the American fintech company Sensible Weather is well-known for its heavy rain insurance, which reimburses same-day travel expenses if it rains during a trip contrary to the forecast. If rain occurs for more than two hours between 8 AM and 8 PM during a trip, compensation is automatically provided without requiring a separate claim, resulting in high customer satisfaction. The company also plans to introduce "heat wave insurance" that covers 100% of travel expenses if temperatures exceed 40 degrees Celsius. Meanwhile, domestic insurance companies aim to launch index-based flight delay insurance by 2024, compensating for delays or cancellations caused by abnormal weather. If an international flight is delayed by more than two hours, a predetermined amount will be paid based on the length of the delay. This initiative is expected to pave the way for a range of index-based insurance products addressing various climate risks.

The arrival of the climate welfare era

The public sector is the final area in which climate sensitivity is essential. Recently, there has been a growing trend to reassess social policy systems through a climate lens, ensuring they reflect climate sensitivity. This includes prioritizing environmental policies that reduce greenhouse gas emissions and expanding facilities that immediately address climate challenges, such as heat shelters, shaded crosswalks, and warm/cool bus stop seats. Moreover, there is an increasing urgency for a true leap into the climate welfare era by implementing policy support that enables

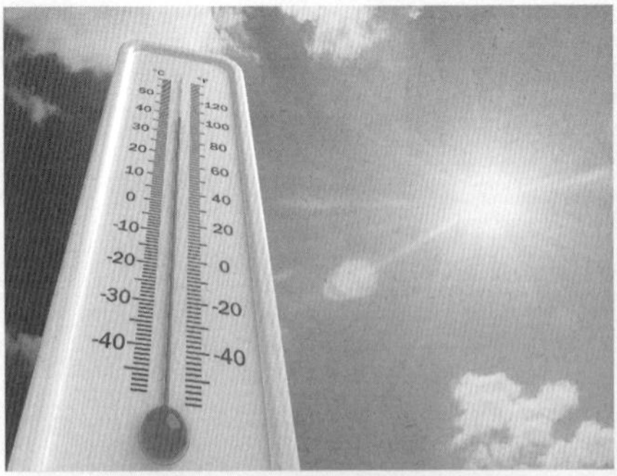

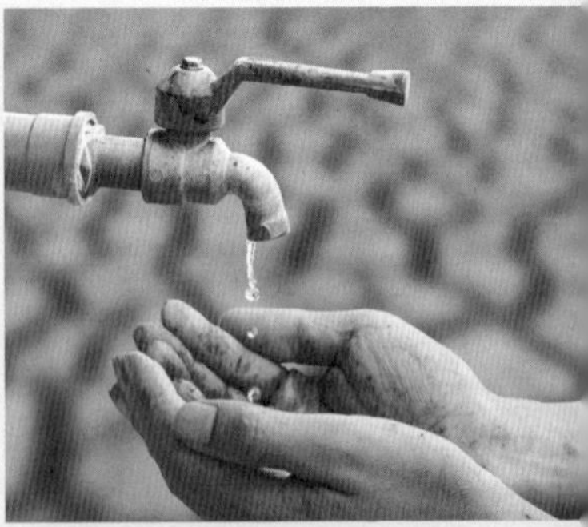

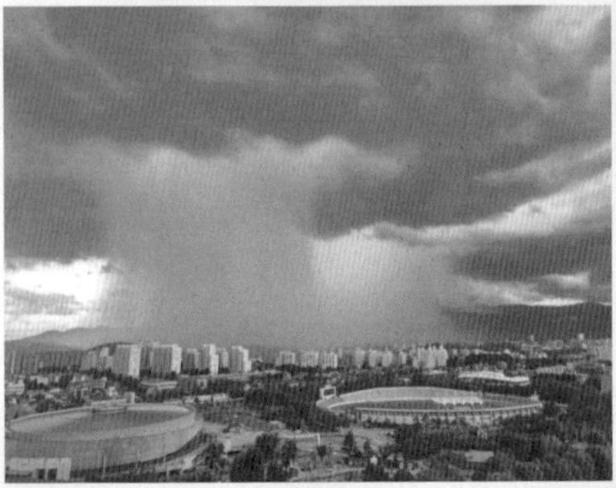

출처: 온라인 커뮤니티 블라인드 갈무리

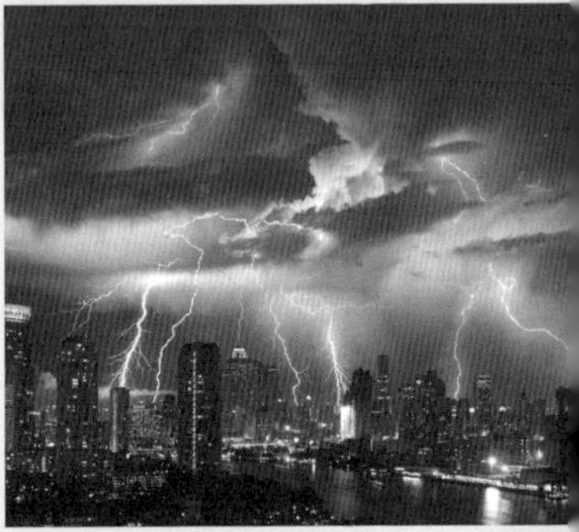

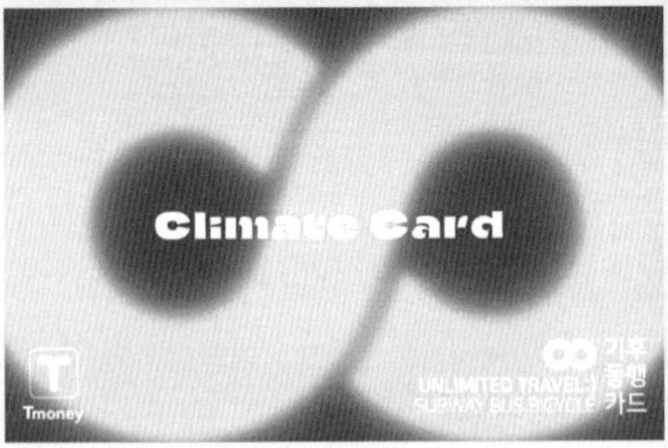

출처: 서울특별시

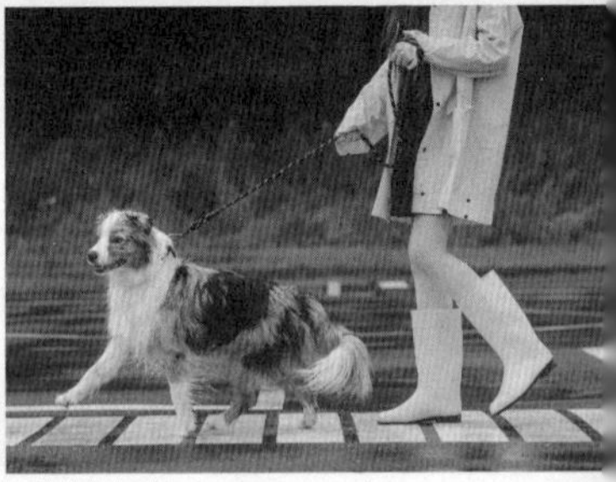

- Global warming is now over.
- We must survive on a boiling planet.
- An enormous challenge has been placed upon 8 billion people.

individuals and businesses to adapt and thrive in the face of the climate crisis.

First, various long-standing social standards are being reconsidered. For instance, it's being suggested that the term *jangma*장마, which has referred to the summer monsoon season for 500 years, be replaced with *ugi*우기, which is the literal Sino-Korean word for "rainy season." This change is proposed because recent years have seen more frequent unpredictable localized heavy rains, resembling a subtropical rainy season rather than the traditional monsoon. At last year's Korean Meteorological Society conference, it was noted that "as the climate crisis deepens, even meteorological perspectives on the monsoon pattern are evolving," leading both the Korea Meteorological Administration and academic circles to carefully consider a change in terminology. Additionally, Arbor Day식목일, traditionally observed on April 5th, is also under review. Climate change has caused summers to start earlier, resulting in earlier blooming periods. The National Institute of Forest Science notes that the optimal temperature for planting seedlings is 6.5°C, but recent Arbor Day temperatures have averaged 11.9°C, a significant increase. In light of this, some are proposing March 21st, recognized by the United Nations as the "International Day of Forests", as a new date for Arbor Day.

The public sector is also actively developing and supporting innovative technologies to combat the climate crisis. For instance, the Korea Water Resources Corporation한국수자원공사

recently showcased their cutting-edge "digital twin" technology at the World Water Forum, which creates a virtual replica of the real world. This allows for the simulation of various real-world scenarios, enabling optimal decision-making on water management issues such as floods, droughts, and water quality. This technology offers a new solution to address abnormal climate patterns that deviate from traditional models. Similarly, the National Institute of Forest Science is developing systems to predict and mitigate risks associated with large-scale forest disasters, which are becoming more frequent due to climate change. One such innovation is the "long-term forest fire risk forecast장기 산불 위험예보," which predicts the likelihood of forest fires one month in advance. This forecast leverages AI to analyze 34 years of accumulated forest fire and weather data, demonstrating high accuracy. The effectiveness of this system was evident in the spring of 2024, a season that previously saw large-scale forest fires annually; thanks to this technology, no major fires occurred, and the area affected by forest fires was reduced to just 1.6% of the previous year's affected areas.

Various policies are being proposed to safeguard society from extreme weather. To protect workers' health, the Ministry of Employment and Labor has introduced a plan to shift workplace heat wave standards from ambient temperature to perceived temperature. This adjustment accounts for the fact that perceived temperature rises with increased humidity, even when the actual temperature remains the same. Given that the UN's International

Labor Organization has warned that 70% of workers globally will be exposed to heat waves, the ministry is actively providing guidance for vulnerable industries and occupations, such as recommending breaks based on perceived temperature levels and suspending outdoor work during extreme heat. Additionally, discussions are emerging about "climate unemployment benefits," which would protect the livelihoods of workers in industries like courier and delivery services by subsidizing a portion of their wages when they are unable to work due to climate disasters. As incidents of work-related injuries and losses due to heavy rain rise sharply, these issues are becoming a focal point of social debate.

Above all, the climate crisis is closely linked to the lives of vulnerable groups, necessitating prioritized attention and preparation. This is evidenced by recent data. The *Climate Crisis Vulnerable Children's Housing Environment Survey*기후위기 취약계층 아동 주거환경 조사, conducted by the Korea Green Foundation환경재단 in early 2024, revealed that 74.3% of low-income children reported changes in their housing environment due to the climate crisis. Specifically, they cited experiences of heat waves, cold waves, increased pests from abnormal temperatures, and more frequent flooding and mold from heavy rain. This indicates that many children require climate welfare support. Similarly, Gyeonggi Province announced it will be the first in the nation to implement a "climate insurance" subscription support project for all residents, with plans to provide enhanced coverage, particularly for vulnerable groups.

Outlook & Implications: A Group Task for 8 Billion People

The climate crisis is my concern

"The addiction has now spread to millions of people around the world, who find they cannot live without cheap cold air."

– from Jeff Goodell's The Heat Will Kill You First

Do you see climate change as your problem? In his book, climate journalist Jeff Goodell highlights that while many people rely on air conditioning for comfort, it's not truly a cooling technology but rather a device that transfers indoor heat outdoors. The issue is that this reliance on air conditioning exacerbates the vicious cycle of the climate crisis. The comfort provided by air conditioning can mask the reality of the climate crisis, leading us to not perceive it as our problem. In truth, failing to recognize a crisis as a crisis is the "real crisis."

The recent climate crisis is particularly troubling because it manifests locally. For instance, this summer, a photo from Wonju in Gangwon Province, showing rain pouring down as if from a hole in the sky, became widely discussed and sparked intense debate on social media. While some speculated it was an AI-generated composite, the reality was that it showed a localized downpour of 70 millimeters per hour. Such localized weather anomalies are often not felt by the broader population, making it easy to dismiss them as someone else's problem. However, their localized nature makes them harder to predict and potentially more damaging, highlighting why climate sensitivity is crucial for everyone.

The climate crisis is undeniably a global issue. We've seen tragic consequences worldwide: an arctic cold wave in California has claimed lives, northern China has experienced 25 large-scale floods, and Antarctica has faced unprecedented heat waves during winter. Climate disasters have become frequent occurrences globally. However, it's striking that South Korea is warming faster than the global average. According to *The Republic of Korea's Adaptation Communication*대한민국 기후변화 적응보고서 , the average annual temperature in South Korea has risen by about 1.6°C over the past 109 years, outpacing the global average increase of 1.09°C. Additionally, sea levels in South Korea have risen more than the global average over the past 30 years. For instance, on July 25, 2024, Seoul recorded a temperature of 32.2°C with 80% humidity, surpassing Bangkok's 30.7°C with 76% humidity. Statements like "Bangkok is cooler than Seoul" or "Let's vacation in Southeast Asia" are not exaggerations.

In response to the escalating climate crisis, some individuals are adopting "prepper" lifestyles, focusing on survival strategies for potential large-scale climate disasters. Preppers are people who anticipate disasters or catastrophes and stockpile food and equipment in preparation. This trend has been growing due to increasing climate concerns. They assemble small survival backpacks with freeze-dried foods, canned goods, and emergency medications, and even construct underground bunkers. Reflecting this trend, Costco in the U.S. has recently begun offering emergency food kits with a 25-year shelf life. These kits include 150 servings of easy-to-prepare meals that only require water and are priced at approximately 110,000 won. The kit has gained popularity on social media, earning nicknames like "Doomsday Meal Kit" and "Apocalypse Kit."

Climate risk management becomes crucial

The World Economic Forum releases its *Global Risks Report* annually, which details current and long-term risks facing the world. This report evaluates threats to the global economy across five areas: economy, environment, geopolitics, society, and technology, and categorizes them by urgency – short-term, medium-term, and long-term. The *Global Risks Report 2024* highlights "extreme weather" as the foremost global risk factor for both this year and the next decade, a shift from last year's report which ranked the "cost-of-living crisis" due to war as the top concern. According to the report, 66% of respondents identified "extreme weather" as the risk most likely to precipitate a global economic crisis, suggesting that climate change could trigger various crises including resource shortages and international conflicts. The report also forecasts that certain parts of the Earth's ecosystem may reach critical climate tipping points within the next 10 years.

These results indicate that addressing the climate crisis extends beyond the scope of a few environmental organizations. Companies, particularly those whose survival depends on maintaining sales, must now prioritize responding to the climate crisis as a pressing threat. Beyond integrating ESG principles, such as reducing carbon emissions and using renewable energy, "climate risk management" is becoming more and more crucial. This involves identifying and preparing for various issues that may arise from extreme weather events. For instance, the U.S. government recently announced that, starting in 2026, companies will be required to estimate and disclose not only their greenhouse gas emissions but also potential damages from natural disasters like floods and wildfires. Such regulations highlight that natural disasters, which have become more frequent due to abnormal climate patterns, are increasingly influencing corporate management.

Despite this, many companies remain focused on immediate performance, and few are fully demonstrating climate sensitivity. It is essential to recognize that future climate changes could pose severe risks to normal business operations, such as unexpected floods disrupting factory production, large-scale weather disasters leading to unexpectedly high insurance payouts, or worsening weather conditions causing raw material supply disruptions.

Some companies are already taking significant steps to prepare for climate crises affecting their major facilities and equipment. For instance, steel manufacturer POSCO faced a major emergency in 2022 when record-breaking heavy rain and river overflow from Typhoon Hinnamnor led to the flooding of most of its plants, resulting in the first-ever shutdown of its factories. Despite employees working around the clock to restore operations, which were normalized in 135 days (faster than anticipated), POSCO incurred losses of up to 2 trillion won. In response, POSCO has since installed a 1.9 kilometer water barrier, set up a real-time water level monitoring system, and is preparing a comprehensive disaster response plan, including the creation of a company-wide disaster response headquarters that reports directly to the CEO.

Similarly, Naver has undertaken meticulous preparations to ensure its data center is protected from various disasters. The company analyzed the soil and geological make-up of potential sites to choose the most suitable location and implemented a special-grade earthquake-resistant design capable of withstanding a magnitude 9 earthquake. This has resulted in a data fortress designed to be resilient against any disaster, reflecting Naver's proactive approach to future climate challenges.

The key to climate action: Clear incentives

The climate crisis is both an individual and collective challenge that requires widespread cooperation. To foster climate sensitivity among many people, clear incentives, even if modest, are crucial. A prime example of this is the Climate Card기후동행 카드 program, an unlimited transit pass introduced by the Seoul Metropolitan Government. This card offers unlimited use of the subway, bus, and Seoul Bike따릉이 (a public bike-sharing service) for 30 days, aiming to reduce climate change by cutting down on private car use. By providing clear financial incentives, the program effectively motivated climate action, with numerous social media posts analyzing the benefits of using the card. Due to these incentives, the Climate Card sold 1 million units in just 70 days and led to a reduction of approximately 100,000 passenger cars over four months, cutting greenhouse gas emissions by 9,000 tons.

Today's climate crisis is often referred to as the "8 billion people's group project," emphasizing that everyone on Earth must collaborate to address it. While we face a tremendous challenge, we also have many solutions at our disposal. To tackle the warming planet, consumers need to engage in proactive climate action, companies must adopt sustainable management practices, and society must prepare for a climate welfare era. As we approach the crucial milestone of 2025, heightened climate sensitivity across all sectors is essential for navigating and thriving in the evolving environmental conditions.

Strategy of Coevolution

공진화 전략

As products and services become increasingly interconnected, it is growing more challenging for a single product to stand out in the market. In today's economy, where interconnectivity is prevalent, it is vital to pursue collaborative growth not just within the same industry but across different industries. With these changes in mind, we will discuss the trend of businesses forming ecosystems and growing together by using the concept of coevolution found in natural ecosystems.

Coevolution can be categorized into "closed-open coevolution," which depends on the number of participants and their openness, and "rigid-flexible coevolution," which depends on the flexibility of participants' roles and relationships.

Survival of the fittest dictates that only those who adapt will endure. Humanity, despite its vulnerabilities, has dominated the planet by continuously evolving in response to environmental changes. The same principle applies to business. In a constantly changing economic ecosystem, coevolution is a necessary strategy. What is most essential is an open-minded approach that allows for flexible and open responses to rapidly shifting market conditions, fostering bold cooperation even amidst competition.

Samsung Electronics and LG Electronics, long-time competitors in the global home appliance market, have teamed up. They now enable their smart home apps to control each other's products. This means you can use Samsung's SmartThings app to operate an LG air conditioner or LG's ThinQ app to manage a Samsung air purifier. However, this collaboration isn't just limited to these two companies. The Home Connectivity Alliance (HCA), an IoT platform association, is gradually building a standardized home appliance ecosystem involving 15 global companies, including Samsung, LG, General Electric, Haier, and Electrolux.

The partnership between Samsung and LG, along with their cooperation within an alliance of 15 global home appliance competitors, would have been unimaginable in the past. So, what made this "sleeping with the enemy" scenario possible? In the modern networked economy, connectivity between products and services is crucial. Previously, excelling in one car model might have been sufficient, but with the rise of electric vehicles, compatibility in charging systems became necessary. Similarly, as autonomous driving technology advanced, the need to share driving data and seamlessly connect with smartphones became paramount. In today's highly interconnected economy, it's vital to pursue growth through close cooperation not only within the same industry but also across different industries. As a result, even traditional rivals are finding it essential to collaborate and expand the market together.

Given these environmental shifts, we would like to discuss the trend of businesses pursuing open ecosystems and growing together by applying the concept of "coevolution" from natural ecosystems. Previously, the term "ecosystem" was primarily associated with entities like the "Apple ecosystem" or "Android ecosystem." However, today, the concept of ecosystems – both large and small – is relevant across almost all industries, making it essential for businesses to collaborate, grow, and evolve together. "Coevolution," a term from biology, describes how multiple species within an ecosystem influence each other and evolve collectively. In a narrow sense, it refers to genetic mutations, while broadly, it encompasses trait changes between species throughout the evolutionary process. This concept is increasingly applicable in the business world, where the mutual influence and growth of companies are known as the "coevolution strategy."

A classic example of coevolution in nature is the relationship between plants and insects. When flowers bloom, insects like bees pollinate them, and when the activity of insects aligns with the flowering period, their feeding activities are maximized, leading to coevolution. Charles Darwin famously hypothesized that an orchid in Madagascar with an unusually long nectar spur must have a corresponding insect with an equally long proboscis. This was confirmed after Darwin's death, validating his theory. Coevolution is an evolutionary process where organisms, such as symbiotic pairs, hosts and parasites, or even predators and prey, influence each other's development. It includes not only cooperative and altruistic evolutionary relationships but also competitive and exploitative ones. For instance, predators may evolve to become more efficient hunters, while their prey simultaneously evolve better defenses to evade them, exemplifying the concept of coevolution in an ecosystem.

Business strategist James Moore introduced the concept of business ecosystems to describe the increasingly dynamic interconnections among companies. In 1993, he articulated this idea in the *Harvard Business Review* as follows:

Successful businesses are those that evolve rapidly and effectively. Yet innovative businesses can't evolve in a vacuum. They must attract resources of all sorts, drawing in capital, partners, suppliers, and customers to create cooperative networks. [...] I suggest that a company be viewed not as a member of a single industry but as part of a business ecosystem that crosses a variety of industries. In a business ecosystem, companies coevolve capabilities around a new innovation: they work cooperatively and competitively to support new products, satisfy customer needs, and eventually incorporate the next round of innovations.

As Moore highlights, a phenomenon akin to biological co-evolution is unfolding in the business world. A natural ecosystem consists of a community of living organisms interacting with their environment, while a business ecosystem represents a market economy environment where multiple companies compete, cooperate, and converge. Much like in a biological ecosystem, participants in a business ecosystem must coevolve, depending on – yet competing with – each other for survival. This process ultimately creates a coevolutionary ecosystem that drives innovation in customer value. Let's delve into the coevolutionary strategies that companies, from small businesses to large corporations, implement within the business ecosystem to secure their survival and success.

Direction and 4 Stages of Coevolution Strategy

Stage 1: Closed self-sufficient system

When a company adheres to a closed policy, ensuring that only its products and services are compatible within its ecosystem, it operates under what is termed a "closed self-sufficient system." Apple serves as a prime example of this strategy, having created a self-contained ecosystem centered around the iPhone, which includes various hardware, software, app stores, and cloud services. This approach is not unique to Apple, as many companies historically aimed to create their own "universe" of products and services. However, Apple stands out for having successfully built a self-sufficient ecosystem that others aspired to but often failed to achieve, thanks to its strong product lineup and intense customer loyalty.

Despite its success, Apple's closed system has recently come under significant scrutiny. In March 2024, the U.S. Department of Justice filed an antitrust lawsuit against Apple, challenging the closed ecosystem it has meticulously developed since the iPhone's launch in 2007. The lawsuit claims that Apple's business practices, which tightly integrate its accessories, music, finance, and apps exclusively with its devices, effectively block other companies from entering the market. This closed strategy, the lawsuit argues, has created an environment incompatible with third-party services, diminishing consumer convenience and stifling the entry of innovative companies into the market.

Legal pressure on Apple is transforming what was once a rigid, closed ecosystem into an opportunity for greater openness. For instance, starting in 2024, Apple plans to allow applications to be installed on iPhones and iPads within the EU without going through its own App Store. Previously, despite criticism from competition authorities in the EU and the U.S., Apple had restricted app installations to its App Store alone. However, this decision comes in response to the EU's Digital Markets Act, which strengthens regulations to curb monopolistic practices by big tech companies.

This shift highlights that while a closed ecosystem might be viable in the market, it may not always be legally sustainable. It signals a broader trend toward enforcing a coevolution strategy that encourages more open participation from various entities, setting a new standard for the future.

Stage 2: Limited partnership

A "limited partnership" occurs when two or more independently operating companies join forces to create growth opportunities together. This type of partnership, which involves a limited number of participants on equal terms, results in a narrower scope of coevolution compared to the more expansive "open cooperation network" discussed later.

One notable example is the collaboration between an automobile company and an appliance company. Samsung Electronics and Hyundai Motor Company are partnering to develop a Car-to-Home and Home-to-Car service that connects homes and vehicles. In the future, Hyundai cars will be able to integrate with Samsung's SmartThings app, allowing drivers to remotely control home devices like air conditioners, robot vacuums, or TVs from their vehicles. This seamless connection could eventually extend beyond electronic devices to include mobile phones and smartwatches, potentially linking to health care solutions that detect drowsy driving and prevent accidents. For Samsung, this partnership presents an opportunity to leverage the automotive platform, expanding its home appliance ecosystem into vehicles.

This trend of limited partnerships is also gaining momentum in the traditionally conservative financial industry. Major U.S. banks like Wells Fargo, Bank of America, and JP Morgan Chase, typically competitors, are collaborating to create a joint electronic wallet. This wallet enables customers to make online payments directly from their bank accounts without relying on third-party payment services like Apple Pay or PayPal. This partnership exemplifies how competitors can cooperate to counterbalance Apple Pay's push into the retail finance market.

In South Korea, similar partnerships are forming between traditional financial institutions and fintech companies such as Kakao Pay. In 2024, Kakao Pay launched a product called "Walking Savings" in collaboration with Jeonbuk Bank and partnered with Lotte Card for joint marketing efforts tailored to Kakao services. While traditional financial institutions seek to strengthen their digital finance sectors by collaborating with fintech companies, fintech firms gain valuable insights from the established experience of traditional banks. Traditional financial institutions are looking to fintech companies for their platform expertise, while fintech companies are partnering with established banks to enhance service visibility and user convenience, benefiting from the experience and regulatory knowledge of their traditional counterparts.

Partnerships are not limited to large corporations; they can also develop between small merchants in local markets and small to medium-sized enterprises. Gwangjang Market in Seoul serves as a prime example of this. With a rich 120-year history, Gwangjang Market is undergoing significant transformation through collaboration among various shops. Established by market vendors in 1905, Gwangjang Corporation currently manages and operates the market building. The corporation has introduced a Starbucks as a new landmark and created a toy museum that showcases an array of figures and toys. Additionally, an unused space has been revitalized into a hub for otaku culture, emphasizing a retro sensibility. The coexistence of traditional shops alongside contemporary concepts has turned the market into a vibrant destination for Gen MZ.

Similarly, Yeongdo in Busan was once noted for its declining population but is now witnessing a remarkable transformation due to an expanding local business ecosystem. As reported by the Korea Tourism Organization, Yeongdo attracted 1.62 million tourists by June 2023, which is 15.1 times the local population of Yeongdo-gu (107,000). This influx of visitors has surpassed consumer spending in Haeundae, Busan's primary tourist area. This success can be attributed to strategic collaborations among local entrepreneurs and business owners since 2021. Visitors taking photos in trendy locales like local food branches and grocery stores have sparked a positive feedback loop, encouraging shopping and visits to the nearby Bongrae Traditional Market.

In Japan, entire neighborhoods have also formed partnerships, striving to create a "neighborhood-wide hotel." This

concept involves integrating existing amenities – such as restaurants, cafes, and shops – into a cohesive ecosystem. In the quaint
shopping district of Fuse in Higashiosaka, Osaka Prefecture,
vacant stores have been transformed into guest accommodations,
inviting visitors to immerse themselves in the local culture,
effectively turning the area into one hotel. While the guest rooms
feature modern interiors, the old signboards remain, preserving
the nostalgic character. Fuse appeals particularly to younger
generations eager to experience the charm of the Shōwa era. The
front of the hotel, once a women's kimono shop, has accommodations that were previously an old confectionery, physical
therapy center, and tea house. Guests are offered packages that
allow them to engage with the local lifestyle, including breakfast
at the traditional *kkikchajeom*끽차점 (Japanese tea house), dinner at
a local *izakaya* or *yakisoba* restaurant, and evening relaxation
in a nearby bathhouse with a 60-year history. This arrangement
provides a rich local experience for guests while benefiting small
local businesses. The total number of rooms is small at 19, yet
5,438 people stayed there as of 2023. When it first opened in
2018, there were 310 guests, but this number has increased 18-
fold in just five years.

Step 3: Open cooperative network

For a company to effectively manage its supply chain and deliver
seamless services, it must establish a smooth cooperative network with other businesses. In the coevolution paradigm, supply

chain management becomes very open, which we will refer to as an "open cooperative network." Previously, building a solid supply chain was crucial; however, in the context of coevolution, it now actively involves companies that share competitive relationships and foster close connections with small startups assuming new roles.

Earlier, we mentioned the collaboration between Samsung and LG in the smart home sector. Notably, when Samsung Electronics launched its 4K OLED TV in Korea in 2023, it drew attention for using LG Display's OLED panels. In the context of South Korean corporate culture, it is rare to source components from a competitor. However, Samsung Electronics signed an agreement to obtain approximately 5 million OLED panels from LG Display over the next five years. This collaboration aligns with Samsung's need to diversify its supply chain and LG Display's goal of increasing profits through OLED sales. Retaining Samsung Electronics, the world's top seller of TVs, as a loyal customer will significantly boost LG Display's profits, while Samsung is expected to enhance its performance centered on premium products like QLED and OLED. Furthermore, the awareness that restraint is necessary in light of the increasing presence of Chinese display companies in the OLED market facilitated this partnership.

As the number of startups with diverse ideas grows, they also play a vital role in the cooperation network. For instance, SK Ecoplant partnered with the eco-friendly startup With M-Tech위

드엠텍 to develop a technology that manufactures cement using industrial waste, reducing carbon dioxide emissions by over 25% in the process. Lotte World is collaborating with the AI startup mAy'I메이아이 to develop a theme park analysis algorithm that monitors customer queues, estimates waiting times, and analyzes queue sections using image processing technology. Large companies are increasingly turning to startups for innovative improvements to their products and services.

The concept of an open cooperative network also applies to R&D. Traditionally, R&D has been a closed domain, as it involves the company's future. However, relying solely on internal resources leads to lower success rates and inefficiencies. Consequently, R&D has evolved into Acquisition and Development (A&D), which involves acquiring external technology and knowledge. This includes purchasing technology or patents when internal capabilities are insufficient. Recently, Connect and Development (C&D) has been emphasized.

C&D involves integrating all external knowledge, ideas, and technologies that can enhance a company's existing capabilities. For example, the Connect + Develop team of P&G (Procter & Gamble) actively seeks out external partners, including startups, laboratories, research institutions, and academia, to create innovative products and solutions that meet the needs of P&G's diverse business divisions. This collaboration exemplifies co-creation, which goes beyond simple outsourcing and significantly contributes to P&G's innovation and sales growth.

This approach is particularly pressing in the pharmaceutical industry, where R&D is critical. New drug development requires substantial time and investment, often taking over 10 years and costing up to 1 trillion won, with a mere 0.01% success rate from candidate exploration to approval. In 2015, German pharmaceutical company Merck established the Merck Innovation Center to be utilized by its employees, startups, and external innovators. The goal is to surpass current technologies by integrating resources and expertise from various fields. Innovative entities, including Merck employees and startups selected through accelerator programs, collaborate to generate new ideas and develop them into new businesses. This exemplifies creating an open network of cooperation through coevolution.

Step 4: Coevolutionary ecosystem

Just as all elements of nature unite to create a single ecosystem, the final stage of coevolution involves various business entities collaborating to form a cohesive "coevolutionary ecosystem." A prime example of such an ecosystem is "open source." As mentioned earlier, Apple faced legal challenges for its highly closed approach, while the Android OS camp, in contrast to Apple's iOS, adopted an open platform strategy. Traditionally, Android has been known for its openness, allowing anyone to participate in the development of knowledge and technology. To enhance this openness, Google established the "Open Handset Alliance," enabling various companies and operators to develop a standard operating system for mobile devices. This approach emphasized an open platform as a means for latecomers to Apple to distinguish themselves from market leaders.

Participants in this alliance include Google, Intel, Qualcomm, Nvidia, Motorola, Samsung Electronics, and LG Electronics, all contributing to the coevolution of the Android platform. Thanks to Google's commitment to openness, anyone can access the Android source code, enabling widespread participation and product development. Ultimately, the ability of smartphone manufacturers to create their own operating systems and advance smartphone evolution stems from the power of open source.

Recently, the concepts of "No Code" and "Low Code" have emerged, building on the open-source model. "No code" refers to developing applications without traditional coding, while "low code" simplifies programming tasks so that individuals with minimal coding knowledge can perform tasks similar to developers. Instead of complex programming, non-developers can create applications through intuitive commands like clicking, dragging-and-dropping, or using voice inputs. By reducing the coding process, development work becomes easier, and developer efficiency increases. As no-code and low-code platforms gain traction, the overall flexibility and speed of coevolution will significantly improve.

Open ecosystems are gaining significant traction in the artificial intelligence market. OpenAI, the creator of the AI chatbot ChatGPT, has launched a GPT store where users can customize

- Charles Darwin was right.
- Google vs. Apple, open vs. closed systems—
  who will win?
- What fun is it if I thrive alone?

 VS.

ChatGPTs to meet their specific needs and share them with others. Any paid subscriber can create a tailored ChatGPT or utilize someone else's version. There is growing anticipation that numerous transformative AIs will emerge in this global AI marketplace. Even Apple, known for its exclusivity, has announced a partnership plan with OpenAI to integrate ChatGPT in 2024. While Apple has traditionally restricted its Siri voice assistant to operate only on the iPhone, it has connected with ChatGPT to enhance information processing when Siri's capabilities are limited. This move maximizes user convenience and enables the GPT store to integrate into the Apple ecosystem, allowing both parties to benefit greatly.

LG has been particularly active in the open-source trend, with its AI Research Institute deciding to release its latest AI model, EXAONE 3.0, as open source. This decision will enable academia, research institutions, and startups to freely access cutting-edge generative AI technology, fostering the development of an open AI research ecosystem.

Currently, an open platform is becoming essential for the creation and innovation of new ecosystems. In line with this trend, Naver is transforming its video service platform, Naver TV, into an open platform where anyone can create a channel and participate, similar to YouTube. Previously, users needed at least 100 subscribers on other platforms like YouTube or blogs to open a channel on Naver TV. Now, the ecosystem is being broadened to encourage short-form content creators.

As highlighted, the coevolution ecosystem strategy is particularly crucial in the IT sector but is also gaining importance in traditional offline industries. In the medical field, for instance, efforts to enhance the interconnectivity of healthcare ecosystems, eco-friendly business ecosystems, small business ecosystems, local business ecosystems, and startup ecosystems are noteworthy. As medical services extend beyond traditional institutions to include non-medical providers, demand is shifting from patients to the general public, creating service areas focused on pre-diagnosis, health maintenance, and monitoring in addition to treatment. Startups like Literacy M aim to empower patients to manage their personal health records across various institutions and to build an integrated medical ecosystem based on ICT infrastructure. In the future, the healthcare sector is expected to expand its ecosystem beyond medicine into diverse non-medical fields, forming a coevolutionary ecosystem that includes industries such as fashion (smart clothing), distribution (health food and pharmaceutical delivery), biopharmaceuticals (genetic diagnosis), finance (insurtech), and electronics (wearable devices).

Outlook and Implications

As industries evolve and become more interconnected, the relationships between companies grow increasingly complex and intertwined. To foster innovation, it is crucial to quickly grasp a company's identity, capabilities, and value while preparing meticulously for collaboration. This means actively seeking practical avenues for mutual benefits, even with competitive or adversarial firms, and building future-oriented trust for co-operation. Here are some key considerations for advancing our coevolution strategy.

First, an innovative ecosystem must effectively integrate business and knowledge ecosystems. The knowledge ecosystem emphasizes knowledge and technology creation, while the business ecosystem focuses on customer value generation. When these two areas are effectively linked, the foundation for innovation becomes stronger. If the knowledge ecosystem is akin to a researcher, the business ecosystem serves as the executor. True innovation occurs when these domains are interconnected and structured. For instance, IBM and MIT collaborate closely to build an innovation ecosystem, establishing a long-term partner-ship and the MIT-IBM Watson AI Lab to accelerate AI technol-ogy development and utilization. Through this partnership, they share knowledge across various AI fields, including machine learning, computer vision, natural language processing, and robotics, creating a cooperative model for joint problem-solving.

While it is essential to engage in a new open ecosystem that facilitates coevolution, it is equally important not to linger on the periphery. Companies should strive to become keystone players within the ecosystem. If even one keystone is removed, the entire structure can collapse. By positioning ourselves as a keystone company within the corporate ecosystem, we can command the ecosystem's dynamics like Google or OpenAI.

The coevolution strategy from an ecosystem perspective is not only vital for large corporations but also essential for addressing local economies and small businesses. Success now hinges not on how exclusivity is built but on the ability to open up and create opportunities for coevolution, where all players can thrive together. Achieving coevolution allows for simultaneous growth of participating companies and consumer satisfaction. In a rapidly changing business environment influenced by customer preferences, technology, and value, the coevolution strategy is poised to become a powerful tool.

Survival of the fittest: only those who adapt will thrive. The reason humanity has dominated the planet is its ability to continuously evolve in response to environmental changes. The same principle applies in the business realm. Coevolution is a vital strategy in today's ever-changing ecosystem. We must move beyond the binary mindset that views competing companies solely as adversaries. Most importantly, we need an open mindset that encourages bold cooperation while competing with each other.

Everyone Has Their Own Strengths:
One－Point－Up

As *Pengsoo* wisely noted, "Everyone is definitely good at something. Just do it better." These days, office workers are shifting away from emulating great figures and putting in long-term effort, opting instead to identify and refine their individual strengths, gradually fostering a sense of accomplishment. This approach, known as "one-point-up," represents a new paradigm of self-development. It emphasizes setting a single, achievable goal and working steadily towards it, preserving one's unique identity.

The essence of one-point-up lies not in adhering to a generic success formula, but in discovering one's own path to success. Instead of overhauling oneself through drastic change, the focus is on improving one specific area today. By documenting and sharing these efforts, individuals can enhance their sense of accomplishment and inspire each other. In an era marked by uncertainty since the COVID-19 pandemic, people are increasingly valuing small, manageable improvements over risk taking. In a time that cherishes stability and incremental progress, the goal is to master small routines rather than pursue extraordinary growth. With job markets often favoring specialized skills over generic qualifications, it is crucial to identify and cultivate your unique strengths. Begin building your value through consistent, small efforts.

원포인트업

W hat are the primary concerns of young office workers today? Marriage? Childcare? Investment? Buying a house? According to the trend hunter group "Trenders Day 2025" from the *K-Consumer Trend Insights* series, the focus is shifting towards career development.

Many workers express the following concerns:
- *"So many technologies are evolving so rapidly; I feel like I can't keep up."*
- *"I'm worried about which direction to take over the next 10 years."*
- *"I need to focus on accumulating skills rather than just following a career path."*
- *"I'm torn between what I want to do and what I must do."*

For over 15 years, *Consumer Trend Insights* has managed a trend hunter group named "Trenders Day트렌더스날," comprising young professionals in their 30s and 40s across various industries. They regularly report on emerging trends and share their recent worries or concerns. In early July 2024, during the Trenders

Day workshop, career development emerged as the predominant concern, despite other issues like real estate, home ownership, parental retirement, relationships, financial investments, and children's education.

Most members of Trenders Day are high-performing professionals, yet their primary worry revolves around career management and development. This isn't merely about job performance, the desire to quit, or workplace difficulties. The crux of their concerns is a strong desire for self-improvement.

This sentiment is echoed by a survey conducted by Job Korea, titled *The Current Status of Career Management for Office Workers,* which polled 1,164 office workers. An overwhelming 87.5% reported having career-related concerns, with over 85% of workers in their 20s, 30s, and 40s expressing similar worries. This indicates that career concerns are prevalent among nearly all workers in Korea, regardless of age.

Indeed, the drive for self-improvement is intrinsic to everyone. People naturally strive to achieve more and to develop incrementally through persistent effort. The desire for self-growth is fundamental; individuals instinctively seek to improve themselves, aiming for a better today than yesterday and an even better tomorrow. This has become particularly pronounced over the past decade.

While self-development and career management have long been topics of interest, the approach to personal growth has evolved significantly. The impact of COVID-19 and the rise of artificial intelligence have fundamentally altered work dynamics, causing fluctuations in self-development trends beyond the simple concept of a "human upgrade업글인간."

Historically, success followed a well-recognized formula: students aimed for prestigious universities, job seekers pursued professional qualifications or sought positions at major companies, and career progression was marked by faster promotions than peers. Role models played a crucial role, with individuals emulating the success formulas of those deemed successful. Common qualifications, such as prestigious degrees and high test scores, were highly valued. During this era, books like *Studying Was the Easiest*공부가 가장 쉬웠어요 and *The 7 Habits of Highly Effective People* frequently topped the self-improvement bestseller lists.

The approach to self-improvement today has shifted significantly. First, success criteria are now highly personalized. Unlike the past, where success often meant adhering to a uniform formula modeled after others, contemporary success is defined individually. Rather than finding a single "right answer," people are now focused on crafting their own unique definition of success.

Second, modern self-improvement emphasizes focusing on achievable, specific goals. Previously, self-improvement aimed at broad, long-term transformations, such as those outlined in Stephen Covey's *The 7 Habits of Highly Effective People*, which advocates for comprehensive life changes from "taking charge of your life" to "continuously renewing" oneself. Today, people have learned through experience that transformative change can't be achieved merely by reading a book. Instead, they prefer setting and achieving smaller, short-term goals, aiming to make incremental progress through manageable steps.

The final element of contemporary self-development is to document and share daily efforts taken, not for social media validation, but for personal reflection and mutual support. The goal is to visually track the progress of your small daily efforts, share them with like-minded individuals, and foster a supportive network.

Reflecting these trends, *2025 K-Consumer Trend Insights* would like to introduce the keyword phrase "one-point-up." This concept represents a new paradigm in self-development: achieving success while maintaining your identity by setting and pursuing a single, achievable goal. Unlike previous self-development approaches focused on dramatic leaps, one-point-up emphasizes gradual, qualitative improvements. It's about evolving slowly and steadily, like a plant that grows by consistently absorbing sunlight and nutrients, rather than seeking immediate, large-scale changes.

The Most Authentic Growth: Just One Level Up

1. Finding the growth point that fits you

The well-known quote from EBS character *Pengsoo* – "Everyone is definitely good at something. Just do it better" – resonates deeply with young office workers today. It underscores the essence of one-point-up: understanding oneself and pursuing growth goals that are uniquely personal. In an era of rapid change and decreasing certainties, the only constant is oneself. By knowing who you are, you establish a firm center, allowing you to navigate life proactively and confidently.

This shift towards finding what suits you rather than adhering to universal success formulas reflects not only the value young people place on individuality but also changes in the hiring land-scape. Historically, large companies used "open recruitment공채" to hire many candidates based on a single standard. Today, "special recruitment특채" for specific roles is preferred, and there is a growing emphasis on "culture fit," which aligns candidates with the company's organizational culture. In this evolving en-vironment, understanding your own characteristics is crucial for effectively targeting the right opportunities and enhancing your chances of success.

This growing interest in personal styling services highlights a broader trend. Even those who aren't public figures are seeking advice on styles tailored to their individual needs. A July 2024 survey by Embrain Trend Monitor found that 46.5% of respon-dents in their 20s, 36% in their 30s, and 30.5% in their 40s have utilized personal styling consultations. These services offer rec-ommendations on colors and fashion that best suit clients' body types and skin tones.

Online personal consulting services, such as Rarelee레어리 and Sherlock Beauty셜록뷰티, are particularly popular. Rarelee operates exclusively on weekday mornings, while Sherlock Beauty offers consultations once a month, with high demand making reservations challenging. These services provide clients with valuable insights through personalized reports, enhancing self-understanding and allowing individuals to better recognize and express their unique identities.

The approach to coaching and mentoring within companies is evolving to emphasize personal development. Today, it's common for department executives to engage in one-on-one coaching with employees each season. This shift reflects employees' desire to understand their roles, strengths, and areas for improvement within the organization.

Rather than solely addressing organizational issues, coaching is now seen as a catalyst for individual growth. Although some may view individual coaching as having limited direct impact on the overall organization, companies are increasingly adopting it due to the demand for personalized, one-point improvement. With younger employees no longer expecting lifetime job security from their employers, they seek support to excel in their current roles. Consequently, individual coaching has become a strategic tool that benefits both employees and organizations by enhancing performance and personal development.

Employee career development often includes job changes. Employees view these transitions not as "quitting" but as a step forward, building on the experience gained at their company. To support this, various resources like resume and self-introduction consultations, interview preparation assistance, and occasionally even financial aid are offered. For example, Patagonia, Inc. is known for conducting exit interviews where employees review their initial hiring interview, reflecting on why they joined, the experiences they anticipated, those they actually gained, and any that were left unmet. This gives the company candid feedback, while allowing departing employees to revisit their original passion and leave with positive memories. By doing this, the company aims to support employee career growth, helping them enhance their skills and pursue career differentiation.

People who don't find opportunities for advancement within their company often seek mentors from outside. Instead of opting for lengthy and costly consulting services, many turn to fast and efficient platforms like Coffee Chat커피챗. Coffee Chat offers career consulting through 20-30 minute conversations on the dedicated app. It connects individuals who may not know each other, fostering the informal culture of coffee chats about work, often seen in IT hubs like Pangyo-dong in Seongnam, Gyeonggi Province. Mentors can create profiles with brief introductions, and those seeking advice can select a topic, industry category, and mentor. The non-face-to-face format of these scheduled calls reduces pressure, allowing participants to ask one or two simple questions or get feedback on portfolios or resumes. Its popularity stems from being a low-cost way to receive helpful advice.

2. Gradually building small achievements

The next key aspect of one-point-up is the steady accumulation of small successes. Once you've identified a growth point that suits you, it's time to make incremental changes. Instead of rushing toward a lofty goal, the focus should be on accumulating small wins and progressing step by step. Just as you move forward by concentrating on the next step rather than the distant finish line, you adapt to uncertainties and keep advancing little by little. With one-point-up, the emphasis is on the "one," i.e., the small, manageable step.

Efficiency is central to one-point-up. It reflects the desire to achieve the most feasible results within a limited amount of time and effort. In a rapidly changing world, it's natural to seek ways to produce visible results with minimal investment. What stands out is the consistent effort aimed at a modest goal. Even if changes aren't immediately noticeable, the focus is on creating a routine centered around the process of small growth.

A routine brings daily renewal and energy. Establishing a personal routine also shows that you're not stuck in a rut. Neuroscientist Dr. Andrew Huberman emphasizes the importance of renewing and revitalizing your life through daily routines. He notes that it's hard to maintain a routine if the goal is solely tied to rewards. Instead, the routine itself – its process – should be the main objective. The same principle applies to small habits. While these habits may not directly lead to grand achievements, the sense of accomplishment from practicing just one habit today is crucial. This feeling of accomplishment is key to maintaining motivation.

When building a career, setting small, achievable goals is crucial. Instead of enrolling in costly, time-consuming courses at academies or institutes, people now prefer to learn specific, essential skills in a shorter time. This has led to the rise of "talent trading" platforms, where individuals can acquire tailored skills from expert mentors or advanced professionals. According to Shinhan Card Big Data Research Institute, the number of users on major talent trading platforms like Soomgo숨고, Kmong크몽, and Tal-ing탈잉 increased by 30 percent in the first half of 2024 compared to the same period in 2022. Transactions on these platforms tend to be small, averaging around 100,000 won, with users seeking help in areas like video editing, hair and makeup, or interview preparation. They aim to invest minimal time to enhance their careers, particularly those in their 20s and 30s, who see these platforms as places to gain the skills they need through "one-point lessons."

A similar trend is emerging in the self-development book market, where smaller, more personal narratives are gaining popularity. Traditional self-help books, often centered on "life skills," used keywords like "without fail반드시," "fast빨리," "rich부자," "certainty확실," "success성공," "already이미," "win이기다," "victory승리," emphasizing goal-oriented success and the drive to achieve grand results, such as "making millions in real estate" or "retiring through stocks." Today, however, micro-content focused on individual experiences is more in vogue. While these achievements may seem minor from a broader perspective, they carry meaning because they represent progress, no matter how small. The focus is on improvement, however incremental, and finding satisfaction in doing just one more thing that you can today.

The concept of one-point-up is also evident in beauty and body care. Treatments aimed at brightening dull skin tones or reducing fine wrinkles are gaining popularity because they are time-efficient, cost-effective, and deliver immediate results. For those hesitant about surgeries requiring anesthesia, hospitalization, or incisions, less invasive techniques such as lasers, high-frequency waves, ultrasound, and injections offer a natural and easy alternative. These methods are minimally invasive and align with the desire for efficiency.

This efficiency-driven trend is also drawing more men to dermatology clinics. Consistent care is key in skincare, but for many busy Korean men, the time commitment has been a major obstacle. Now, treatments like laser therapy and injections that show noticeable results in just one or two hours are reducing that barrier. According to Shinhan Card Big Data Research Institute, men's spending at approximately 3,300 dermatology clinics nationwide is projected to rise by 36% in 2024 compared to 2020, outpacing the growth in women's spending. This highlights the importance of maintaining a youthful appearance as a form of self-investment for men as well.

The same logic of small but consistent effort applies to fitness. In a time-strapped society, brief yet effective exercises are gaining attention. Research suggests that lifting dumbbells at maximum strength just once a day can significantly build muscle, and short two to five-minute walks after meals help regulate blood sugar levels. Additionally, engaging in activities that get your heart rate up for one to two minutes during daily tasks can dramatically lower the risk of death from cancer or cardiovascular disease, even without setting aside dedicated exercise time.

3. Consistently record and share through your network

The third key to one-point-up is consistent recording and sharing. This isn't about showing off or seeking recognition from others. Instead, it's about motivating yourself through the support and encouragement of those around you. By documenting and sharing your progress, you can visually reaffirm your goals and small achievements.

Recording and sharing is like looking in a mirror; it allows you to objectively assess yourself, notice small improvements from yesterday, and set a course for the future. It helps reignite motivation when you're feeling lazy or on the verge of giving up. You only truly notice change when you can see it, and growth becomes continuous when you can feel it. Most importantly, daily recording provides a sense of control, giving you confidence that you are managing your life effectively. This sense of "visible change" makes recording and sharing vital elements of the process.

Many people use diaries for this purpose. One popular option is the "self-questioning" diary by Indigo인디고, a stylish stationery brand. This diary prompts self-discovery through 100 thoughtful questions. The process of reading and answering these questions gives you a chance to reflect on fundamental aspects of your identity. Questions like "Who am I?" may feel too grandiose, but simpler queries such as "What kind of expression do I have these days?" allow for gradual self-exploration. To answer, you must metaphorically (or literally!) look in the mirror and consider whether you like what you see, and what kind of expression you wish to have. The future is shaped by a clear understanding of the present. This shows that "future you" is not a distant, different person, but a natural continuation of who you are now.

Blogs and YouTube are also popular platforms for recording and sharing daily life with others. According to a survey on personal network management conducted by Job Korea and Albamon in August 2024, 18.3% of people in their 20s reported managing their personal network through personal branding activities, such as operating YouTube channels or blogs, more than any other age group. These two platforms have a common feature: they enable individuals to express themselves and connect with others through content. Blogs offer the freedom to articulate thoughts, experiences, and talents through writing, while YouTube allows for visual storytelling through videos. Both serve as stepping stones for building deeper relationships by showcasing individuality and personal stories, potentially creating new op-portunities.

In addition to these digital platforms, some people join themed groups or "mission bands." These groups focus on shared activities like writing, walking 10,000 steps a day, or drawing, where members can participate, record their progress, and encourage each other to achieve their daily goals. This creates a sense of community and accountability in pursuing personal growth.

With 887,000 subscribers as of August 25, 2024, "The Pri-vate Lives of Today's People요즘사, yozmsa is a popular YouTube and podcast channel that focuses on sharing the possibilities and real-life examples of living authentically. The channel features a diverse range of interviewees, including a painter who also works as a cleaner and individuals who have quit multiple jobs and embraced frequent career changes. These guests are not following the conventional path but are instead practicing "a life true to oneself," rejecting societal expectations in favor of their own authentic experiences.

What makes the channel resonate with viewers is its candid discussions about the personal choices made by these individuals in various life situations. The honesty of these stories allows viewers to reflect on their own circumstances, often leading them to ask, "What choice should I make in my situation?" This relatability and openness are key to the channel's widespread popularity.

Background: Survival Strategy in an Era Where Grandeur Has Disappeared

"Oh! You've planned everything in advance!"

This line from *Parasite* is perhaps one of the most memorable in the film. Why did it resonate so deeply with people? Likely because it has become so difficult to make plans in this world. In a time when plans change daily, the audience connected with the character Ki-taek (played by Song Kang-ho) when he said, "The most perfect plan is no plan." This reflected a growing realization: uncertainty has made life unpredictable and beyond control.

Uncertainty means it's hard to foresee outcomes or maintain control, and this has been exacerbated by rapid societal changes. The pinnacle of unpredictability was the COVID-19 pandemic, which blindsided the world and proved impossible to manage in advance. After experiencing such an unexpected, uncontrollable event, people began to understand that creating large, long-term plans is often futile. What matters is surviving day to day, with the only things we can truly control being "myself" and "my present." This shift in mindset underpins the rise of the one-point-up trend, where the focus is on achieving small, manageable goals in the immediate here and now.

The concept of one-point-up shares similarities with the #VOD trend mentioned earlier, particularly in its context. In a modern society where every day feels like a struggle, and people find themselves grateful for a peaceful day without problems, envisioning grand dreams can be challenging. Perhaps one-point-up represents a self-development approach that aligns well with the #VOD era. In such times, prioritizing "peace of mind" takes precedence over seeking "overwhelming emotion" or "extraordinary growth." The sense of stability that comes from knowing that you are not stuck in a rut is often enough.

The tendency to avoid risks has also contributed to the emergence of the one-point-up trend. Even with perfectly crafted life goals, unexpected events like international economic shifts can derail those plans. In a rapidly changing work environment influenced by advancements in artificial intelligence, accumulating qualifications that may soon lose their value feels increasingly futile. We have witnessed promising skills become obsolete in just a few years. In this context, focusing on small, attainable goals becomes far more significant than taking unnecessary risks.

As society grows more uncertain, finding reliable role models has become increasingly difficult. In the past, older individuals with experience imparted wisdom, offering models of success and guidance to younger generations. However, in our fast-paced world, the value of existing experiences and knowledge has diminished. Age and experience no longer guarantee the right path. We now find ourselves in an era where "reverse mentoring," where younger individuals guide their elders, is gaining traction. As uncertainty in life escalates, people tend to forge their own paths and define their achievements rather than relying on traditional role models. Instead of unattainably aspiring to become superstars, individuals are more inclined to engage with colleagues who share similar concerns, focusing on actionable steps they can take.

In addition to these social changes, the one-point-up trend is closely tied to the evolving workplace culture that office workers are experiencing. In an interview, Yoon Soo-young, CEO of the book club startup Trevari트레바리, noted that "while there was considerable interest in 'side jobs' to diversify income streams around 2021, during the financial technology boom, there is now a stronger focus on enhancing one's capabilities within one's current job." This shift arises from the challenges of securing additional income through side jobs, particularly in a stagnant economy and a deteriorating investment environment. The on-going low-growth trend has led many to believe that improving performance in their current roles is more prudent than seeking new employment opportunities.

The once-popular notion of the "Great Resignation" era has now transformed into the "Great Retention" era. However, remaining at a company doesn't mean simply coasting along; individuals are expected to grow by at least one incremental step in their skills and contributions.

The belief that goals are meaningful solely for their aspirational value, even if unachievable, is now outdated. We are no longer in an era of chasing dreams regardless of their feasibility. Instead, we find ourselves in an era of only dreaming those dreams that *are* feasible. People seek to improve their performance just a little, maintain the status quo, and strive to be slightly better than they were yesterday.

Outlook & Implications

So, how should we respond to the one-point-up era, and how is this trend likely to evolve in the future? Let's examine this from both organizational and individual perspectives.

Organizations need to rethink their talent development strategies. Customized growth support has become crucial. Rather than relying on a one-size-fits-all education program, companies should implement tailored mentoring and coaching initiatives that align with individual capabilities and goals. Providing employees with opportunities for self-directed growth is essential.

For instance, Coupang has introduced a program within its engineering organization that accepts applicants every quarter. Individuals with various roles, including developers, planners, designers, technical PMs, data scientists, and business analysts, can apply. Participants have the flexibility to take on roles as mentors, mentees, or both, depending on their needs. If they seek mentorship in a specific area, they can request it directly. To maximize the program's benefits for everyone involved, mentors and mentees are thoughtfully paired. After pairing, the program offers a range of helpful guidelines and tips throughout the three-month mentorship period, ensuring a supportive and productive experience for all participants.

On an individual level, employees should embrace the one-point-up philosophy by identifying and focusing on small, achievable goals that can contribute to their personal and professional development. This may involve seeking out new skills, exploring mentorship opportunities, and actively participating in growth programs offered by their organizations.

As this trend continues to develop, we can expect a greater emphasis on continuous learning and adaptability. Individuals who prioritize their growth within their current roles will not only enhance their own capabilities but also contribute positively to their organizations. Ultimately, the one-point-up trend encourages a shift towards a more sustainable and realistic approach to personal and professional development, allowing both organizations and individuals to thrive in an ever-changing environment.

Amazon's approach to mentorship is noteworthy. The company provides members the opportunity to receive mentoring in a flexible format and at their preferred times through an internal mentoring program platform. This platform connects employees with various experts across the organization, regardless of geographic location. At Amazon, any member can become a mentor or mentee, promoting a rich exchange of knowledge. Even if a mentor's expertise isn't directly related to the mentee's current role, employees can select individuals with specialized skills or relevant experience who can assist in their career growth.

Participants can choose their desired mentor, but the platform also uses an AI algorithm to suggest suitable matches. This algorithm considers factors such as career paths, job roles, positions, specialties, and locations, ensuring that mentees are paired with mentors who can best support their development. By fostering such a dynamic mentoring environment, Amazon exemplifies how organizations can adapt to the one-point-up trend, enhancing employee growth and satisfaction while cultivating a culture of continuous learning.

Recently, the focus on in-house human resource development has shifted from simply managing the organization to fostering the growth of individuals. Organizations must now guide members to share their goals and grow together. Previously, success was defined by becoming an executive through hard work, emphasizing hope and sacrifice. Today, leadership focuses on motivating individuals and groups to set and achieve goals. In the one-point-up era, policies and support must leverage individual strengths. As past knowledge and experience become less relevant due to rapid changes, even employees in their 50s or older need new growth opportunities. Organizations should convert individual efforts into collective momentum, fostering voluntary motivation, encouraging small changes, and empowering members to advance.

Empathy for individual experiences is also crucial. Instead of highlighting success stories or grand goals, content should offer practical motivation and comfort through daily effort and growth processes. For instance, Simmons has named its department focused on employee growth and organizational performance "Growth Design," reflecting the belief that member development ensures organizational sustainability. Meeting members' growth needs will contribute to the long-term success of the organization.

The one-point-up trend poses challenges for all of us who aspire to grow. Most importantly, we must recognize that our careers – rather than just our jobs – are becoming paramount. In this era, what we are responsible for is more significant than where we work. Whether we switch jobs or retire early, continuously developing our skills is crucial for our livelihood.

To achieve this, individuals should adopt a strategy akin to that of a "strong small business강소기업." This term refers to a company that prioritizes solid technology or products over expansion and marketing, maintaining a sustainable scale it can manage. This approach mirrors the current aspirations of individuals. While striving to be better than yesterday is essential, attempting to emulate others can be overwhelming and unmanageable. Thus, it is vital to cultivate one's unique strengths and actively work on enhancing them to achieve excellence.

One-point-up is a form of self-affirmation that emphasizes being true to oneself. Unlike the past, when the focus was on expansion, the emphasis now is on self-awareness and being present. In a society that feels unstable and where preparing for the future can be daunting, it is essential to pause and turn our attention inward.

One-point-up is not merely about accumulating skills or knowledge; it's about recognizing and accepting oneself in the present moment. It involves celebrating small successes, refraining from frustration over failures, and embracing who we are. One-point-up is about seeking a daily change of just 1% in our current state. While 1% seems negligible, the compound effect of a steady 1% increase is profound. Multiplying 1 by itself 365 times yields just 1, but multiplying 1 with the added 1%, 1.01, by itself 365 times results in 37.8. Consistent and even minimal effort can lead to extraordinary outcomes. Begin your own journey of practical, one-point-up growth today.

- Do one thing well. Just improve on that.
- Level up just one thing! Don't aim for the stars!
- Focus on short distances, not long ones.
  Concentrate on achievable goals!

Authors

Rando Kim (김난도)

Rando Kim is a professor in the Dept. of Consumer Science (DCS), Seoul National University (SNU). As a specialist in consumer behavior and market trend analysis, he has written more than 20 books including the *Trend Korea* series, *Dining Business Trend* series, *Market Kurly Insight*, *The Hyundai Seoul Insight*, *Trend China*, *What Consumers Want*, and *Luxury Korea*. He also wrote essay books, *Amor Fati*, *Future and My Job*, and *Youth, It's Painful* which have sold three million copies in 17 countries. He has conducted research projects about consumer needs finding, new product planning, and market trend probing for Korea's major companies like Samsung, LG, SK, CJ, Hyundai Motors, GS, LH, Amorepacific, Lotte, Fursys, Nongshim, and Coway.

Miyoung Jeon (전미영)

Miyoung Jeon is a research fellow at the Consumer Trend Center (CTC) under Seoul National University. She holds BA, MA and PhD degrees in Consumer Science. Since 2009, she has co-authored numerous books including the annually published and top-ranked book series *Trend Korea*, as well as *Trend China*, *Dining Business Trend* series, and *Breakthrough Power*. Miyoung worked as a research analyst at Samsung Economic Research Institute, served as a research professor at SNU, and is currently a columnist for *Dong-A Ilbo's* 'Trend Now' section. Additionally, she holds positions as the chair for Lotte Shopping's ESG Committee and serves as an advisor for multiple organizations including LG U+, Hana Bank and the Seoul Metropolitan Government. Currently, she collaborates with various companies, focusing on new trend-based product development and strategic planning.

Jihye Choi (최지혜)

Jihye Choi, PhD in Consumer Science from DCS, SNU, works as a research fellow at CTC. She has participated in many consulting projects with Korea's leading companies such as Samsung and LG, and gives public lectures on consumer trends. She currently teaches consumer behavior and qualitative research methodology at SNU. She contributes many articles and columns to major Korean newspapers and media.

Jung Yoon Kwon (권정윤)

Jung Yoon Kwon currently works as a research fellow at CTC, SNU. She obtained her BA, MA, and PhD degrees in Consumer Science, SNU. She explored the intergenerational transmission of consumption styles in her PhD dissertation. She has participated in many consulting projects with leading Korean companies such as Samsung and CJ, and she also teaches an Introduction to Consumer Science course at Sung Kyun Wan University.

Dahye Han (한다혜)

Dahye Han currently works as a research fellow at CTC, SNU. She received a BA in Psychology, SNU and obtained MA and PhD degrees in Consumer Science, SNU. Her PhD dissertation focused on the structure and measurement of consumption emotions. As a researcher, she received a paper award from the Korean Consumption Culture Association in 2022.

Also, she is conducting a number of consulting projects with major Korean companies, such as Samsung and LG.

Hyewon Lee (이혜원)

Hyewon Lee is a PhD in Consumer Science, SNU and is currently a senior researcher at CTC. She is interested in generation theory and changes in consumer behavior due to technological advances, based on insights gained while working at the Korea Publishing Culture Association, Dasan Books, Reader's Book, and Kakao Page. Recently, she has been conducting research on expanded cultural capital to explore the drivers of consumption trends that cannot be explained by economic capital.

June Young Lee (이준영)

June Young Lee currently works as a professor at Sangmyung University. He received a doctorate degree in Consumer Science, SNU. He received 'The Best Paper Award' in the International Journal of Consumer Studies . He worked as a senior researcher at Life Soft Research lab at LG Electronics. He is a laboratory chief at the Consumer Research Center in Sangmyung University.

Hyang Eun Lee (이향은)

Hyang Eun Lee is an Executive Director at LG Electronics Home Appliance & Air Solution [H&A] Business Division. She holds a Master's degree from Central Saint Martins in the UK and a Ph.D. in Design from Seoul National University.

At LG Electronics, she is responsible for product planning focused on customer experience [CX] innovation. Her work includes launching innovative products, discovering and managing new business models, establishing CX-based management strategies, and designing product and space services. As a professor in the Department of Service·Design Engineering at Sungshin Women's University, she has conducted numerous corporate customer experience projects, bridging academia and industry. She is also actively engaged in research, publishing papers in top 25% [Q1] SSCI and SCIE international journals. As an expert bridging theory and practice, she has been writing a column titled "Lee Hyang-eun's Trend Touch" for the *JoongAng Ilbo* since 2021.

Yelin Chu (추예린)

Yelin Chu received an MA degree in Consumer Science, SNU. Currently, she is attending a PhD program and serves as a senior researcher at CTC. Her Master's thesis was entitled "A Study of Consumer Experience on the Online Education Service with Conditional Tuition Refund." She is interested in analyzing big data to distill insights from unstructured data, and in deriving further meaning from participant interviews through qualitative research.

Dahyen Jeon (전다현)

Dahyen Jeon is currently working on her PhD and is a senior researcher at CTC. She received a BA degree in Fashion Industry at Ewha Womans University and an MA degree in Consumer Science at SNU. She was awarded first place in the Korean Society of Clothing and Textiles (KSCT) contest in 2019. Her area of interest is consumer behavior in the digital retail environment. Her current research focuses on online visual cues and haptic imagery.

Naeun Kim (김나은)

Naeun Kim is currently enrolled in a PhD program and works as a senior researcher at CTC. She earned her master's degree in Consumer Science, SNU. Her master's thesis is titled "*A Study on Small Luxury Consumption*

Motivations and Consumer Typologies." She is interested in analyzing new consumption phenomena in modern society and aims to conduct research that combines qualitative and quantitative approaches that can provide a rich interpretation of consumers' hidden needs and influencing factors.

YouHyun Alex Suh (서유현)

YouHyun Alex Suh holds a Ph.D. in Consumer Science from Seoul National University, an MS in Culture Technology from KAIST, and a BA(Hons) in *Textile Design* from *Central Saint Martins*, London, UK. With a multidisciplinary background in science, art, and the humanities, she brings a unique, creative, and interdisciplinary approach to her work. Her expertise includes quantitative and qualitative research on consumer needs, with a strong focus on trend analysis, design management, consumer behavior, customer experience strategy, and new product planning. She previously worked as a Customer Experience (CX) Specialist at LG Electronics.

2025
K-Consumer Trend Insights

초판 1쇄 발행 2024년 10월 25일

지은이 김난도 · 전미영 · 최지혜 · 권정윤 · 한다혜 · 이혜원 ·
　　　　 이준영 · 이향은 · 추예린 · 전다현 · 김나은 · 서유현
감수 미셸 램블린
펴낸이 성의현
펴낸곳 미래의창

등록 제10-1962호(2000년 5월 3일)
주소 서울시 마포구 잔다리로 62-1 미래의창빌딩(서교동 376-15, 5층)
전화 02-338-6064(편집), 02-338-5175(영업) **팩스** 02-338-5140
홈페이지 www.miraebook.co.kr
ISBN 978-89-5989-725-4 13320

※ 책값은 뒤표지에 있습니다.